The Most Controversial Decision
Truman, the Atomic Bombs, and the Defeat of Japan

This book explores the American use of atomic bombs and the role these weapons played in the defeat of the Japanese Empire in World War II. It focuses on President Harry S. Truman's decision making regarding this most controversial of all his decisions. The book relies on notable archival research and the best and most recent scholarship on the subject to fashion an incisive overview that is fair and forceful in its judgments. This study addresses a subject that has been much debated among historians, and it confronts head-on the highly disputed claim that the Truman administration practiced "atomic diplomacy." The book goes beyond its central historical analysis to ask whether it was morally right for the United States to use these terrible weapons against Hiroshima and Nagasaki. It also provides a balanced evaluation of the relationship between atomic weapons and the origins of the Cold War.

The Reverend Wilson D. Miscamble, C.S.C., joined the permanent faculty at Notre Dame in 1988. A native of Australia, he was educated at the University of Queensland, from which he graduated in 1973, and obtained a master's degree three years later. In 1976, he came to Notre Dame to pursue graduate studies in history. He received his doctoral degree in 1980. He then served for two years as North American analyst in the Office of National Assessments, Department of Prime Minister and Cabinet, Canberra, Australia. In August 1982, he returned to Notre Dame and entered the priestly formation program of the Congregation of Holy Cross. He was ordained a priest on April 9, 1988. His primary research interest is American foreign policy since World War II. He is the author of *George F. Kennan and the Making of American Foreign Policy, 1947–1950*, and *Keeping the Faith, Making a Difference*. He has edited *American Political History: Essays on the State of the Discipline* and *Go Forth and Do Good: Memorable Notre Dame Commencement Addresses*. His most recent book, *From Roosevelt to Truman: Potsdam, Hiroshima, and the Cold War*, was published in 2007 and received the Harry S. Truman Book Award in 2008.

Advance Praise for *The Most Controversial Decision*

"This is truly a bravura performance. Wilson Miscamble, in concise, lively, and bare-fisted prose, captures the essence of President Harry S. Truman's decision making regarding the American use of atomic bombs and the roles these weapons played in the defeat of Imperial Japan in World War II. In particular, Professor Miscamble takes aim at the cottage industry of Truman critics who argue that the president employed 'atomic diplomacy' to put the brakes on Soviet ambitions in eastern and central Europe, or lacked insight into the events unfolding around him. Common sense, together with an easy command of the extant documents, leads Miscamble to another conclusion: had Truman 'not authorized the attacks on Hiroshima and Nagasaki thousands of American and Allied soldiers, sailors, marines, and airmen would have been added to the lists of those killed in World War II.' The question he raises has had few takers: 'Could an American president have survived politically and personally knowing that he might have used a weapon that could have avoided their slaughter?' Miscamble's treatment of Truman and the bomb should be the first port of call when scholars want to revisit the most controversial decision taken by a twentieth-century president. This is an ideal text for undergraduate and graduate students alike."

– Joseph M. Siracusa, Royal Melbourne Institute of Technology,
coauthor of *America and the Cold War, 1941–1991:
A Realist Interpretation*

CAMBRIDGE ESSENTIAL HISTORIES

Series Editor

Donald Critchlow, *St. Louis University*

Cambridge Essential Histories is devoted to introducing critical events, periods, or individuals in history to students. Volumes in this series emphasize narrative as a means of familiarizing students with historical analysis. In this series leading scholars focus on topics in European, American, Asian, Latin American, Middle Eastern, African, and World history through thesis-driven, concise volumes designed for survey and upper-division undergraduate history courses. The books contain an introduction that acquaints readers with the historical event and reveals the book's thesis; narrative chapters that cover the chronology of the event or problem; and a concluding summary that provides the historical interpretation and analysis.

Other Titles in the Series

Edward D. Berkowitz, *Mass Appeal: The Formative Age of the Movies, Radio, and TV*

John Earl Haynes and Harvey Klehr, *Early Cold War Spies: The Espionage Trials that Shaped American Politics*

James H. Hutson, *Church and State in America: The First Two Centuries*

Maury Klein, *The Genesis of Industrial America, 1870–1920*

John Lauritz Larson, *The Market Revolution in America: Liberty, Ambition, and the Eclipse of the Common Good*

Charles H. Parker, *Global Interactions in the Early Modern Age, 1400–1800*

The Most Controversial Decision

Truman, the Atomic Bombs,
and the Defeat of Japan

WILSON D. MISCAMBLE, C.S.C.
University of Notre Dame

CAMBRIDGE
UNIVERSITY PRESS

CAMBRIDGE
UNIVERSITY PRESS

University Printing House, Cambridge CB2 8BS, United Kingdom

One Liberty Plaza, 20th Floor, New York, NY 10006, USA

477 Williamstown Road, Port Melbourne, VIC 3207, Australia

4843/24, 2nd Floor, Ansari Road, Daryaganj, Delhi - 110002, India

79 Anson Road, #06-04/06, Singapore 079906

Cambridge University Press is part of the University of Cambridge.

It furthers the University's mission by disseminating knowledge in the pursuit of
education, learning and research at the highest international levels of excellence.

www.cambridge.org
Information on this title: www.cambridge.org/9780521735360

First published 2011

A catalogue record for this publication is available from the British Library

Library of Congress Cataloging in Publication data
Miscamble, Wilson D., 1953–
The most controversial decision : Truman, the atomic bombs, and the defeat of Japan /
Wilson D. Miscamble.
  p.   cm. – (Cambridge essential histories)
Includes bibliographical references and index.
ISBN 978-0-521-51419-4 (hardback) – ISBN 978-0-521-73536-0 (paperback)
1. Hiroshima-shi (Japan) – History – Bombardment, 1945 – Moral and
ethical aspects.   2. Nagasaki-shi (Japan) – History – Bombardment, 1945 – Moral and
ethical aspects.   3. Atomic bomb – History.   4. Atomic bomb – Moral and ethical
aspects.   5. Truman, Harry S., 1884–1972 – Military leadership.   6. United States –
Military policy – Decision making.   I. Title.   II. Series.
D767.25.H6M47   2011
940.54′2521954–dc22

2010045937

ISBN 978-0-521-51419-4 Hardback
ISBN 978-0-521-73536-0 Paperback

To

My Mentor and Treasured Friend
VINCENT P. DE SANTIS
Captain, U.S. Army (19th Regiment, 24th Infantry Division),
who fought in the Pacific War

Contents

Acknowledgments

The idea for this book emerged during a discussion with my friend Donald Critchlow. Subsequently, Don kindly invited me to publish it as a volume in the Cambridge Essential Histories series that he edits. I am indebted to Don for his support of this project, and to both him and his wonderful wife Patricia for their friendship over the years. I am very glad to publish another book with Cambridge University Press. I am deeply grateful to my editors and friends, Lewis Bateman and Eric Crahan, for their encouragement, patience, and generous assistance. Let me also thank Anne Lovering Rounds, Shari Chappell, and Jennifer Carey at Cambridge University Press for all their assistance with the book. Cynthia Landeen prepared the fine index with care and dispatch.

I am especially thankful for the scholarly support extended to me on this project by Michael Kort and Joseph Siracusa, especially in their comments on the draft manuscript and other helpful suggestions. I have drawn on their work and the scholarship of other fine historians whose publications I highlight in the citations and in the suggestions for further reading. I must specifically acknowledge here my substantial intellectual debt to Richard B. Frank and Dennis Giangreco whose important studies guided my work.

This book develops from my earlier study on the implications for American foreign policy of the transition from Franklin Roosevelt to Harry S. Truman, and I remain grateful to all those individuals and institutions who supported me on that project. Let me make special mention of my gratitude to the staff of the Harry S. Truman Library, especially Michael Divine, Sam Rushay, Randy Sowell, Liz Safly, and Lisa Sullivan. Pauline Testerman of the Truman Library staff arranged for the photos used in this book. My friends Steve Brady and Stephen Koeth, C.S.C., again proved to be careful readers of the manuscript drafts. The estimable Bill Dempsey gave me thoughtful comments on Chapter Seven, which I appreciate. My able research assistants Brian Corrigan, Kelly Schumacher, and Stephen Chronister helped me on this book and on a host of other matters, large and small, as they well know.

I began work on this book during a most enjoyable year on sabbatical as a visiting Fellow at the International Security Studies Center at Yale University. I didn't finish the book that year, and that might have been caused partly by the wonderful hospitality of John Gaddis and Toni Dorfman, Sun-Joo Shin and Henry Smith, my confrere John Young, C.S.C., and Reverend Daniel Sullivan and all the good folk at Our Lady of Mt. Carmel Parish in Hamden, Connecticut. Their kindness already has me looking forward to my next sabbatical there!

At Notre Dame I benefit from supportive colleagues and from the notable help of Myrtle Doaks, my coworker in the vineyard, in the History Department office. I am appreciative to be a member of the Moreau Seminary Community at Notre Dame, although I must apologize to my confreres there if the topic of this book has entered too often into my conversation. I am grateful for the support of my various family members in Australia, especially my dear parents and my sister and brother, and for their combined counsel that I "just finish" the book.

This book is dedicated to my mentor and treasured friend, Vincent P. DeSantis, Professor Emeritus of History at Notre Dame, as a mere token of my gratitude to him. I came to Notre Dame to work under his direction thirty-five years ago, and ever since he has been a constant source of encouragement to me in all my endeavors. I want also to pay tribute here to his courageous service in the Pacific War as an officer in the 19th Regiment of the 24th Infantry Division. Vincent occasionally has told mutual friends that he was "in Australia before Bill was." I am glad of this and want to record in print my appreciation of his efforts and those of so many young Americans like him who defended Australia during its darkest hours, and went on to play their part in securing victory in the war against Japan.

Wilson D. (Bill) Miscamble, C.S.C.
Notre Dame, Indiana

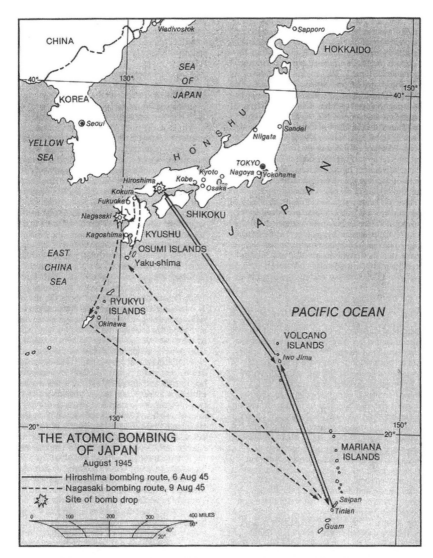

MAP 1. The Atomic Bombing of Japan – Hiroshima and Nagasaki Bombing Routes. Reprinted from Vincent C. Jones, *Manhattan: The Army and the Atomic Bomb* (Washington, D.C.: U.S. Government Printing Office, 1985).

INTRODUCTION

The Most Controversial Decision

The commemoration of the fiftieth anniversary of the dropping of the atomic bombs on Hiroshima and Nagasaki sparked a significant scholarly and popular dispute in the United States. A bevy of books appeared wrestling with questions concerning the necessity, the wisdom, and the morality of America's use of the new weapon in 1945.[1] An even more inflammatory and public controversy centered on the text developed to accompany the planned exhibit at the Air and Space Museum of the Smithsonian Institution of a part of the fuselage of the *Enola Gay*, the American B-29 aircraft that dropped the atomic weapon on Hiroshima on August 6, 1945. Supposedly reflecting the most recent scholarly findings and self-consciously unafraid to puncture prevailing national "myths," the Smithsonian text gave a privileged voice to an interpretation that held that the atomic bomb was not necessary to either end the Pacific War or to save American lives. The predictable public outrage apparently caught the Smithsonian curators by surprise. The historian J. Samuel Walker recounted that "veterans' groups led a fusillade of attacks that accused

[1] A sample of the works published around the fiftieth anniversary includes Gar Alperovitz et al., *The Decision to Use the Atomic Bomb and the Architecture of an American Myth* (New York, 1995); Robert James Maddox, *Weapons for Victory: The Hiroshima Decision Fifty Years Later* (Columbia, MO, 1995); Robert Jay Lifton and Greg Mitchell, *Hiroshima in America: Fifty Years of Denial* (New York, 1995); Robert P. Newman, *Truman and the Hiroshima Cult* (East Lansing, MI, 1995); and Stanley Weintraub, *The Last Great Victory: The End of World War II, July–August 1945* (New York, 1995). The more recent sixtieth anniversary passed in more subdued fashion with a mere flurry of op-ed pieces and magazine articles published in early August 2005. For the best of these, see Richard B. Frank, "Why Truman Dropped the Bomb," *The Weekly Standard*, 10 (August 8, 2005), pp. 20–25.

the Smithsonian of making the use of the bomb appear aggressive, immoral, and unjustified."[2] With considerable congressional support, the aging veterans, members of the proverbial greatest generation, forced the Smithsonian to back down, to modify the text considerably, and to alter the thrust of the exhibit. This led in turn to lengthy lamentations that blatant political pressure had censored a well-researched, historical presentation.[3]

The commotion surrounding the *Enola Gay* exhibit ultimately generated much more heat than light. It proved to be just another in a long series of disputes and debates that has made the use of the atomic bombs without doubt President Harry S. Truman's most controversial decision. At base these debates arose out of a rejection of the arguments put forth by policy makers like Truman and his Secretary of War Henry L. Stimson that the atomic bomb "obviated the need for an invasion of Japan, accelerated the conclusion of the war, and saved a vast number of American lives."[4] Especially after the appearance of Gar Alperovitz's *Atomic Diplomacy* in 1965, various writers increasingly challenged the notion that the atomic bombs were needed to defeat a Japan that supposedly stood very close to surrender. Alperovitz has been nothing if not consistent, and in his massive book marking the fiftieth anniversary of the bomb's use he reiterated his contentious thesis along with its corollary that the Truman administration used the atomic weapons as part of its diplomacy aimed primarily at the Soviet Union.[5] As one close observer of the atomic debate noted, Alperovitz's work "redirected the focus of questions that scholars asked about the bomb." Instead of attending to the necessity of the bomb, "the central questions had become: What factors were paramount in the decision to use the bomb and why was its use more attractive to policymakers than other alternatives."[6] This seemingly subtle change of emphasis in

---

[2] J. Samuel Walker, "The Decision to Use the Bomb: A Historiographical Update," in Michael J. Hogan, ed., *America in the World: The Historiography of American Foreign Relations Since 1941* (Cambridge and New York, 1995), p. 206.

[3] For further details of the Smithsonian controversy told largely from the perspective of those sympathetic to the originally planned exhibition, see Edward T. Linenthal and Tom Englehardt, eds., *History Wars: The* Enola Gay *and Other Battles for the American Past* (New York, 1996). For a more critical treatment of the exhibit, see Robert P. Newman, "*Enola Gay* at Air and Space: Anonymity, Hypocrisy, Ignorance," in Robert James Maddox, ed., *Hiroshima in History: The Myths of Revisionism* (Columbia, MO, 2007), pp. 171–189.

[4] Walker summarizes this position in his "The Decision to Use the Bomb," p. 207.

[5] See Gar Alperovitz, *The Decision to Drop the Bomb and the Architecture of an American Myth.*

[6] Walker, "The Decision to Use the Bomb," p. 213.

effect put the Truman administration on trial for its use of the powerful new weapons. Why had it done what wasn't really necessary went the reasoning implicit in this approach.

The questions a historian asks hold great importance and influence significantly how well any explorer of the past can map and understand its difficult terrain. In such contested and controversial territory as the use of the atomic bombs, it seems wise to clarify at the outset the questions that this book addresses and seeks to answer. Essentially, it examines why the bombs were used at Hiroshima and Nagasaki, and then goes on to investigate the role they played in Japan's surrender. Pursuing these fundamental matters allows for other fascinating questions to be addressed. Would Truman's great predecessor, Franklin D. Roosevelt, have used the atomic bombs in the manner that Truman authorized? Did the likely possession of the atomic bombs transform American military calculations as the Pacific War came to an end, and alter American intentions toward its then Soviet ally? Were the Japanese really on the verge of surrender before the atomic bombs were used? Should the bombing of Hiroshima be seen as the opening salvo in the Cold War as Gar Alperovitz suggested so provocatively more than forty years ago? How is the Potsdam conference (July 17–August 2, 1945), Truman's one and only exercise in Big Three summitry, related to America's possession of the atomic bomb? Answers to such questions help shed light on the crucial issue regarding the necessity of using these terrible weapons to force Japan's defeat.[7] These matters are surely the province of the historian and might reasonably suffice in an effort to understand Truman's decision making and its consequences. Yet, given the intensity of the conflict surrounding the atomic bomb, it seems essential to also confront the question regarding the morality of the atomic bomb. Thus, this book explores whether it was right for the United States to use this weapon against Hiroshima and Nagasaki. I find convincing the observation of the Yale historian John Lewis Gaddis that one "can't escape thinking about history in moral terms" and rather than doing this implicitly or subconsciously I prefer here to engage the issue explicitly.[8] I trust my analysis might instigate good reflection and discussion among my readers.

I have not sought to engage in any detailed refutation of the work of other historians, although this book assuredly revises and directly

---

[7] See the very helpful chapter on "Key Questions and Interpretations," in Michael Kort, *The Columbia Guide to Hiroshima and the Bomb* (New York, 2007), pp. 81–116.

[8] John Lewis Gaddis, *The Landscape of History: How Historians Map the Past* (New York, 2002), p. 122.

challenges certain past interpretations. Rather, my effort here takes account of the available and extensive documentary evidence on this much debated issue, and it draws on the best scholarship on the subject. It also seeks to take into account the most recent work on the use of the atomic bombs. The continuing appearance of new studies testifies to the enduring effort to understand and explain the American bombing of Hiroshima and Nagasaki.

The effort in this book to understand and explain Truman's decision to use the atomic bombs draws heavily on my earlier book *From Roosevelt to Truman: Potsdam, Hiroshima, and the Cold War*.[9] In that book I made a genuine effort to treat Truman as more than a one-dimensional figure. I sought to reveal him as the more complex man he truly was – one blessed with certain strengths and beset with notable limitations, who was occasionally given to uncertainty and indecision on matters of foreign policy. Understanding this more complicated figure allows for a deeper appreciation of his foreign policy and his decision making. So too does a firm grasp of the circumstances in which he operated. This book, like *From Roosevelt to Truman*, accepts the complexity, the uncertainty, the sheer messiness of policy making. It tries to convey the tense atmosphere in which policy makers worked, the heavy pressures they endured, and the complex of influences that weighed upon them. I trust it will lead readers to better understand Truman and his most controversial decision.

---

[9] Wilson D. Miscamble, *From Roosevelt to Truman: Potsdam, Hiroshima, and the Cold War* (New York and Cambridge, 2007).

CHAPTER I

Franklin Roosevelt, the Manhattan Project, and the Development of the Atomic Bomb

Harry Truman bore the ultimate responsibility for the use of the atomic bombs, but the American decision to develop these weapons for use in World War II was made by Franklin Roosevelt. Truman's predecessor is a dominant political figure of the twentieth century. His place in American history rests secure as a great leader in peace and war, a brilliant political practitioner, and the measuring rod for all subsequent presidents. In the depths of depression he helped restore to an almost despairing nation real hope and energy with his New Deal measures. He overcame the powerful forces of American isolationism and unilateralism in the years from 1939 to 1941 and supported Great Britain and the Soviet Union in their deathly struggle against Hitler's Germany. After Pearl Harbor he convinced the American people that they faced a truly global challenge, which required the defeat of both Germany and Japan. He led a unified nation through to the brink of ultimate victory in the greatest armed conflict in history.

Yet, when examining Roosevelt's portrait more closely and beyond the broad brush strokes formed by his buoyant leadership of his nation through the Depression and the Second World War, his picture becomes more blurred. Roosevelt might best be thought of as a remarkable exemplar of the "political fox" in action.[1] He was never limited by any central conviction or purpose. Rather as a "magnificently resourceful improvisor" and "a virtuoso in the use of power" he displayed during the New Deal a

---

[1] See Owen Harries, "The Day of the Fox," *National Interest*, 29 (Fall, 1992), pp. 109–112. Harries's terms are inspired by Isaiah Berlin's famous essay on Tolstoy, "The Hedgehog and the Fox." Also note, of course, James MacGregor Burns's classic study *Roosevelt: The Lion and the Fox* (New York, 1956).

willingness to shift directions and to vary his methods without inhibition as circumstances required. He relied more heavily on the force of his personality than on the force or consistency of his ideas. At times he avoided arduous study of complex issues and chose not to outline detailed plans. This certainly characterized his involvement in the development of the atomic bomb.

While FDR's policy commitments and purposes occasionally proved difficult to pin down, no observer ever doubted his mastery of the White House and his complete comfort with and confidence in his use of presidential power. He dominated all those who served in his administration, and utilized the practices of dividing authority and assigning overlapping responsibilities to pit subordinates against one another and to make himself the locus for all major decisions.[2] Those who wanted to prompt any decisive action by the American government knew they must contact and convince President Roosevelt. So, at least, thought the great physicist and refugee from Nazi Germany, Albert Einstein.

On August 2, 1939, Einstein wrote to Roosevelt that "the element uranium may be turned into a new and important source of energy in the immediate future." Having been briefed on the subject himself by Leo Szilard, a brilliant Hungarian physicist and fellow refugee, Einstein explained further to the American leader that "it may become possible to set up a nuclear chain reaction in a large mass of uranium, by which vast amounts of power and large quantities of new radium-like elements would be generated." Such scientific details were hardly designed to capture the president's interest, but the distinguished scientist assuredly hoped the president would attend to his warning that "this new phenomenon would also lead to the construction of a bomb and it is conceivable – though much less certain – that extremely powerful bombs of a new type may thus be constructed."[3] Einstein offered suggestions to address the broad issue, and asked that a relationship be established between the administration and physicists, like Szilard and Enrico Fermi, a refugee from Fascist Italy and the 1938 Nobel laureate, who were researching these chain reactions. He also requested enhanced funding for the physicists' experiments and for a national effort to secure plentiful sources of

---

[2] Patrick Maney makes this point in *The Roosevelt Presence: A Biography of Franklin Delano Roosevelt* (New York, 1992), p. 191.

[3] Einstein to Roosevelt, August 2, 1939 in Kort, *Columbia Guide to Hiroshima and the Bomb*, p. 172. For a helpful and accessible discussion of "the science of nuclear weapons" see Joseph M. Siracusa, *Nuclear Weapons: A Very Short Introduction* (Oxford and New York, 2008), pp. 2–6.

uranium. Einstein closed his letter by apprising Roosevelt that German scientists also were engaged in work similar to that of Szilard and Fermi, and that Hitler's nation had moved to secure its own sources of uranium. He felt no need to explicate the dangerous implications of this German research.

Despite his great scientific reputation Einstein had no easy entrée to or helpful contacts in the White House. The president only read his letter and discussed it on October 11 when he met with Alexander Sachs, a Wall Street economist and political associate, who served as an intermediary for the scientists. By this time Nazi Germany had attacked Poland and World War II had begun. The president's attention understandably focused on the current crisis, but he referred Einstein's letter to an exploratory committee consisting of Sachs and representatives of the Army and Navy and headed by Dr. Lyman Briggs, director of the Bureau of Standards. This committee reported on November 1 and indicated support for research on whether a chain reaction could produce a bomb. It offered some limited support for the scientists and authorized the modest sum of six thousand dollars to help build what would be the world's first nuclear reactor at the University of Chicago. "These funds," Michael Kort noted, "turned out to be the miniscule down payment for a project that ultimately would cost two billion dollars."[4] It was hardly an auspicious start.

During 1940, American scientists continued their modest and mainly theoretical research in their university laboratories while still afraid that German scientists might steal ahead in a race to build a bomb. Their fears were shared across the Atlantic by scientists in a Great Britain now locked in mortal combat with Nazi Germany and fighting on alone after the fall of France in June of that year. While the fighters of the Royal Air Force held off the *Luftwaffe* in the skies above, British physicists working in crucial collaboration with various émigrés who had escaped the Nazis pursued what they named the Tube Alloys project exploring the feasibility of a bomb. They reached important conclusions regarding the uranium isotope, U-235, and how it might be applied to create a nuclear fission weapon. The British presented the results of their research in the report of the MAUD (incidentally a code name and not an acronym) Committee in July 1941. They spoke to the practicality of constructing the bomb even by the end of 1943, and predicted it would be of decisive importance in the war.[5]

---

[4] Kort, *Columbia Guide to Hiroshima and the Bomb*, p. 17.
[5] On the British efforts see Margaret Gowing, *Britain and Atomic Energy, 1939–1945* (New York, 1964).

Although the United States had still not formally entered the war, the British shared the MAUD report in October 1941 with Roosevelt's science advisers, now led by Vannevar Bush, who directed the Office of Scientific Research and Development. In contrast to Einstein's letter the MAUD report provoked a more high-powered response. Roosevelt now seemed to grasp the danger that German success in producing such a weapon represented. He wrote Churchill to secure further cooperation between the British and American efforts. Soon after the Japanese attack on Pearl Harbor on December 7, and the German declaration of war against the United States four days later, FDR authorized Bush to develop an atomic bomb. By June 1942 Bush counseled the president that the U.S. Army must take over the huge work of constructing the factories and facilities to produce the essential fissionable materials to make the atomic weapons. The U.S. Army Corps of Engineers assigned the project to the Manhattan Engineering District headquartered in New York City, and it became known then and subsequently as the Manhattan Project.

The story of the vast endeavor to produce the atomic bombs has been well told elsewhere.[6] It suffices to say that it brought together the top scientists of the day, including many exiles from Nazi and Fascist Europe, and combined them with the vast productive capability of American industry as applied through companies like the DuPont Corporation. In September 1942 after some troublesome initial months, Brig. Gen. Leslie Groves took command of the Manhattan Project. A hard-driving and determined officer of conservative disposition who had just overseen the construction of the Pentagon building, Groves took literally his instructions from Secretary of War Henry Stimson to produce a bomb "at the earliest possible date so as to bring the war to a conclusion."[7] His deputy later described General Groves as "the biggest sonofabitch I've ever met in my life, but also one of the most capable," and under his relentless direction three major research and production sites were developed at Oak Ridge, Tennessee, Hanford, Washington, and Los Alamos, New Mexico.[8] The first two huge operations focused on producing the materials for a bomb, which by now included not only U-235 but also plutonium (Pu-239), a new transuranic element discovered by the brilliant chemist Glenn Seaborg by bombarding the more common

---

[6] See Richard Rhodes, *The Making of the Atomic Bomb* (New York, 1986); and Richard G. Hewlett and Oscar E. Anderson, Jr., *The New World, 1939–1946*, Vol. I, *A History of the United States Atomic Energy Commission* (University Park, PA, 1962).

[7] Groves quoted in Kort, *Columbia Guide to Hiroshima and the Bomb*, p. 19.

[8] Col. Kenneth Nichols quoted in Rhodes, *The Making of the Atomic Bomb*, p. 426.

PHOTO 1. The so-called odd couple who led the Manhattan Project: Maj. Gen. Leslie Groves and Dr. J. Robert Oppenheimer. (Courtesy Harry S. Truman Presidential Library.)

uranium isotope U-238 with neutrons. The Los Alamos site served as the weapons research and design laboratory to fashion both the U-235 and the plutonium into usable bombs. This was a monumental challenge and ultimate success was at no point fully guaranteed. Yet, it would be there in the New Mexico desert that the first atomic device would be tested three years later.

In mid-October 1942, just weeks after his own appointment, Groves selected a cosmopolitan and sensitive Berkeley physicist of leftist political sympathies named Robert Oppenheimer to direct the Los Alamos

PHOTO 2. Three of the leading scientists at Los Alamos – E. O. Lawrence, Enrico Fermi, and Isidor I. Rabi. (Courtesy Harry S. Truman Presidential Library.)

laboratory. Oppenheimer loved the poetry of John Donne and read the *Bhagavad Gita*, the great Hindu epic, in the original Sanskrit, which left Groves quite unimpressed. Yet, the blunt military officer sensed intuitively that Oppenheimer could lead the diverse and brilliant group of scientists who would be gathered under the umbrella of the Manhattan Project – men such as the Nobel laureates Ernest Lawrence, Enrico Fermi, and Isidor Rabi. As is often noted they made an unlikely match – someone later quipped it was "Godzilla meets Hamlet" – but they developed a formidable partnership.[9] Together they led the massive yet secret effort to build the bomb whose huge costs Roosevelt approved without consulting Congress at all.

Even before Groves and Oppenheimer began pouring their impressive energies and talents into producing a bomb, Franklin Roosevelt and Winston Churchill had held the first of a series of meetings devoted to the atomic bomb project. They met in June 1942 at the president's estate at Hyde Park in New York. There they agreed informally that the effort to build the bomb would be a joint Anglo-American project in which information would be freely shared. The British prime minister expressed his concerns about German progress on the bomb. He knew from British intelligence, which tracked the German effort closely, that German scientists led by the Nobel Laureate Werner Heisenberg were fully engaged in their efforts to capture the power of nuclear fission.[10] Neither the British nor the American leader expressed any significant reservations about the new weapon and, while they never formally approved its use, an operating assumption emerged that if and when it was completed it would be directed against their Nazi foe.

While Roosevelt and Churchill shared this basic working assumption throughout the war, occasional tensions characterized their dealings over the atomic bomb.[11] At their meetings in Casablanca in January 1943 and in June of that year in Washington D.C., Churchill complained forcefully of the lack of cooperation and the failure to provide the British with full access to the Manhattan Project research. At a subsequent 1943 conference held at Hyde Park and then in Quebec City Roosevelt extended assurances about future collaboration thereby rejecting the advice of those among his advisers who favored a more unilateral American approach. The two leaders also agreed that their "mutual consent" would be required to use an atomic bomb, and to share any information about it with a third party.[12] This agreement calmed troubled waters. More British scientists crossed the Atlantic to participate directly in the

---

[9] For the "Godzilla" quip see Andrew Rotter, *Hiroshima: The World's Bomb* (New York and Oxford, 2008) p. 110.

[10] For a good summary of both the German and the Japanese efforts during World War II to build an atomic bomb see Andrew Rotter's, *Hiroshima: The World's Bomb*, pp. 62–83.

[11] For a fine summation of these tensions see Warren F. Kimball, "The Bomb and the Special Relationship," *Finest Hour: The Journal of Winston Churchill*, No. 137 (Winter, 2007–2008), pp. 37–42.

[12] For the Quebec Agreement, August 19, 1943, see Kort, *Columbia Guide to Hiroshima and the Bomb*, pp. 174–175.

Manhattan Project. Additional assistance came from Canada, which primarily provided uranium for the project. The following year Roosevelt and Churchill met again in the familiar environs of Hyde Park and reaffirmed the Anglo-American monopoly over the atomic bomb project. By this point it was clear that any possible weapon would likely not be ready before Germany's defeat. Despite the entreaties of the Danish refugee physicist Neils Bohr, the British and the Americans decided against sharing any information on the Manhattan Project with the Soviet Union. (The Soviets through their Operation *Enormoz* espionage efforts had other sources on it!)[13] Churchill pushed FDR to agree at this Hyde Park meeting in September 1944 to treat the matter "as of the utmost secrecy." They also formally agreed in this discussion on the military use of the weapon. "When a 'bomb' is finally available," their aide-memoire read, "it might perhaps, after mature consideration, be used against the Japanese, who should be warned that this bombardment will be repeated until they surrender."[14]

Roosevelt and Churchill reached other decisions and fashioned other policies that indirectly also contributed in important ways to the eventual decision to use the atomic bomb. At the Casablanca Conference in Morocco in January 1943 FDR took the initiative and, with Churchill's concurrence, announced the policy of unconditional surrender for the Axis powers. There would be no negotiation of terms this time, no possibility for any claims that intact military forces had been stabbed in the back by cowardly civilian officials as had been alleged of the German surrender that ended World War I. Germany and Japan would need to be fully occupied and seriously reformed to uproot effectively the Nazism and Japanese militarism that underlay their rapacious aggression. The unconditional surrender policy gained ready public acceptance. It became an

---

[13] For details of Soviet espionage on the Manhattan Project see Allen Weinstein and Alexander Vassiliev, *The Haunted Wood: Soviet Espionage in America – the Stalin Era* (New York, 1999), pp. 172–222; Nigel West, *Mortal Crimes: The Greatest Theft in History – the Soviet Penetration of the Manhattan Project* (New York, 2004); and John Earl Haynes and Harvey Klehr, *Early Cold War Spies: The Espionage Trials That Shaped American Politics* (Cambridge and New York, 2006), pp. 138–151. Also see the special issue entitled "Soviet Espionage in the United States during the Stalin Era" of *The Journal of Cold War Studies*, Vol. 11 (Summer, 2009).

[14] For discussion of the Hyde Park agreement and Roosevelt's subsequent discussions on the development and control of the atomic bomb see Hewlett and Anderson, *The New World, 1939–1946*, pp. 325–329. Also see Martin J. Sherwin, *A World Destroyed: The Atomic Bomb and the Grand Alliance* (New York, 1975), pp. 108–114.

article of faith that the Germans and the Japanese must be defeated completely and utterly. Harry Truman certainly thought it so.

In pursuing their battle with Hitler up through 1944 and beyond, Churchill and Roosevelt relied heavily on air power aimed not simply at German military targets but also at cities and towns. Here, it was Churchill who led the way. As early as July 1940 in the face of an imminent German invasion of his country, Churchill wondered how Britain might still win the war. He gave his answer in a letter to Lord Beaverbrook, the minister of aircraft production, in which he held that "there is one thing that will bring him [Hitler] back and bring him down, and that is an absolutely devastating, exterminating attack by very heavy bombers from this country upon the Nazi homeland." This was, as Churchill's great biographer later noted, the prime minister "trying to imagine a way that might one day destroy the Nazi juggernaut."[15] Eager to maintain British morale in the face of the German blitz against London and other cities, Churchill authorized bombing raids against German cities including Berlin. The main targets initially were industrial centers and transportation hubs but as the bombing program grew through 1941 and 1942 major cities became the targets. Facing brutally high casualties during their daytime bombing efforts the British turned to nighttime bombing where their planes were less vulnerable to German fighters and antiaircraft fire. Under the command of Air Marshall Arthur 'Bomber' Harris, the British Bomber Command pursued a strategy of "area bombing" aimed at undermining German morale and destroying productive capacity by targeting whole cities and towns. Over the subsequent years Harris ordered upwards of a thousand planes into nighttime bombing raids against specific German cities with little regard for civilian casualties.[16] Despite some reservations from British officials, few serious questions were raised about this harsh strategy. As one astute observer later noted "military necessity was the mother of moral justification."[17] Churchill saw it as stern justice for the people who supported Hitler. He and eventually FDR had firmly established a strategy by the beginning of 1945 where airpower was to be used to the full, although the American Air Force at great cost had persisted through 1944 with its efforts to bomb

---

[15] For Churchill's letter and the biographer's comment see Sir Martin Gilbert, "Churchill and Bombing Policy," *Finest Hour: The Journal of Winston Churchill*, No. 137 (Winter, 2007–2008), p. 28.

[16] Tami Davis Biddle, "Bombing by the Square Yard: Sir Arthur Harris at War, 1942–1945," *The International History Review*, Vol. 21 (September, 1999), pp. 626–664.

[17] Gerard J. DeGroot, *The Bomb: A Life* (Cambridge, MA, 2005), p. 68.

specific military/industrial targets in daytime. Such a strategy easily accommodated the use of an atomic bomb should one be produced.

This readiness to utilize airpower to wreak as much destruction as possible on the hated German and Japanese foes reflected an American approach to war that emphasized achieving "complete victory at the lowest cost in American lives." Roosevelt recalled the massive casualties of World War I when the European powers had virtually decimated a generation of young men in trench warfare. He intended to avoid such carnage among American troops, and wanted the United States to use "its industrial might and technological prowess to reduce the number of casualties it would suffer" on the battlefield. "In winning this war," he explained to a radio audience in November 1944, "there is just one way to guarantee the minimum of casualties – by seeing to it that, in every action, we have overwhelming material superiority."[18] This outlook partly drove the American willingness to invest such vast resources in the Manhattan Project. If technological superiority might be applied effectively to save American lives, Roosevelt believed it should be so used. His successor would think likewise.

At no point did either Roosevelt or Churchill assume that an atomic bomb, if and when completed, would secure by itself the unconditional surrender of Japan. Their grasp of the likely power of the potential new weapon seems to have been limited. Warren Kimball has suggested that "Roosevelt, like most non-scientists, did not comprehend the revolutionary potential of nuclear weapons." He notes that James B. Conant, another of FDR's key science advisers, held that the president had "only fleeting interest in the atom, and that the program never got very far past the threshold of his consciousness." Churchill told Niels Bohr that "this new bomb is just going to be bigger than our present bombs and involves no difference in the principles of war."[19] With their hazy knowledge of the bomb's potential and their uncertainty about whether it would actually fulfill the predictions of their scientific advisers, both men knew they must prepare for conventional military efforts to defeat the Japanese Empire. They also knew that the far larger share of the burden for this challenging undertaking would fall to the United States.

Given the military challenge involved in defeating Japan, FDR eagerly sought the aid of the Soviet Union and assurances from Josef Stalin that he

[18] For the Roosevelt quotation and the earlier quotes see J. Samuel Walker, *Prompt and Utter Destruction*, p. 9.
[19] For all the quotations see Kimball, "The Bomb and the Special Relationship," p. 40.

would enter the Pacific War upon Hitler's defeat. At the Yalta Conference early in 1945, Roosevelt obtained a pledge from Stalin that the Soviets would enter the war against Japan "two or three months after Germany has surrendered and the war in Europe has terminated." Typically, Stalin laid out clear conditions for his entry into the Pacific war. He would gain outright the Kurile Islands and the southern part of Sakhalin, have the status quo in Soviet-controlled Outer Mongolia confirmed, and regain the lease on the naval base at Port Arthur. While agreeing that China should retain sovereignty in Manchuria, Stalin extracted endorsement for a proposal for the joint operation by a Sino-Soviet company of the Chinese Eastern Railroad and the South Manchurian Railroad. Roosevelt cavalierly undertook to gain the concurrence of Chiang Kai-shek for these terms, which effectively conceded to the Soviets a sphere of influence in the region. Stalin, no doubt eager to formalize these favorable arrangements, indicated a willingness to conclude "a pact of friendship and alliance between the U.S.S.R. and China."[20] Throughout his negotiations of this matter, FDR notably treated it primarily as a military concern, and, according to one close student of the episode, "it was apparently on the advice of the Joint Chiefs who viewed the problem in purely military terms ... that he made his decision to pay the price of Soviet intervention."[21] Believing that an invasion of its home islands would be necessary to unconditionally defeat Japan and, as always, eager to minimize American casualties, Roosevelt saw the benefits of a Soviet attack on Japan's Kwantung Army in Manchuria. Perhaps, as Averell Harriman later suggested, Roosevelt also wanted a clear delineation of Soviet desires in the Far East and to assure Soviet support for Chiang's Nationalist government. Whatever the relative importance of these factors, the Yalta Far Eastern Accord constituted an important element of Roosevelt's legacy to Truman and provided some of the geopolitical context for the use of the atomic bomb.

These Far Eastern agreements reached at Yalta were kept a closely guarded secret, of course, but Roosevelt returned from the conference with optimistic assurances for the American people. In retrospect one sees that a vast overselling of the agreements occurred, which heightened public expectations unduly. FDR invited James F. Byrnes, an experienced

[20] "Agreement Regarding Entry of the Soviet Union into the War against Japan," *FRUS: Malta and Yalta*, (Washington, D.C., 1955), p. 984.

[21] Louis Morton, "Soviet Intervention in the War with Japan," *Foreign Affairs*, Vol. 40 (July, 1962), p. 662.

politician, to accompany him to Yalta and the former Senate majority leader hurried back from Yalta and served as FDR's advance man, portraying the conference as the fulfillment of the Atlantic Charter. The treasured principle of self-determination, he reported, remained intact. The publication of certain of the Yalta accords generated much favorable publicity and praise for Roosevelt's accomplishment. On March 1, the president addressed a joint session of Congress on the Yalta meeting in words he knew the legislators wished to hear. He spoke movingly from the well of the House chamber sitting at a desk in what was not so much an admission of his disability but an indication of his physical exhaustion. With Vice President Truman perched behind him and listening intently, he advised that Yalta had laid the foundation for a lasting peace settlement. It might not be perfect, he explained, "but it can be a peace – and will be a peace – based on the sound and just principles of the Atlantic Charter."[22] Heartened by the ringing applause, he petitioned the American people and their representatives to extend their active support for his handiwork.

Roosevelt sought to build strong domestic support for his postwar plans, but he did so by being less than open with his people. The stakes he thought were too high for that. With the ghosts of Henry Cabot Lodge and company haunting him, he feared similar obstructionism from the Senate to that which had bedeviled Woodrow Wilson. Presumably he believed that any admission of the likely limitations of the postwar settlement would be grist for isolationist mills. Arguably, as John Harper has noted, this "was another case of 'useful deceit,'" a circumventing of painful realities in the interests of a supposedly higher good, especially at a time when he believed he needed Soviet support in the Pacific war in order to minimize American casualties.[23] However that may be, Truman inherited a public unable to see through the thin tissue that papered over increasing Big Three divisions and holding firm expectations for continued unity and joint purpose among the major allies. Roosevelt had never truly attempted to educate the American people on the blunt realities of the postwar world order that inevitably would differ significantly from their Wilsonian ideals. That education took place after his death.

While most historians describe Franklin Roosevelt's efforts at Yalta as a further step – for good or ill – in pursuit of his broad vision of great power

---

[22] Samuel I. Rosenman, ed., *Franklin D. Roosevelt: Public Papers and Addresses*, Vol. 13 (New York, 1950), pp. 570–586.

[23] John Lamberton Harper, *American Visions of Europe: Franklin D. Roosevelt, George F. Kennan and Dean G. Acheson* (Cambridge and New York, 1994), p. 126.

cooperation, some, like Arthur Schlesinger and Robert Dallek, detect that he began to reconsider this approach in the months after the conference. In response to the difficulties involved in the implementation of the Yalta agreements on issues such as the composition of a postwar government for Poland, so this view goes, FDR began a reevaluation of his long-held plans. The legitimacy of Roosevelt's second thoughts on his approach to the Soviets seems supported by the fact that he had held back certain arrows in his diplomatic quiver in anticipation of a time when he would need to apply pressure on Stalin and adopt more of a quid pro quo approach. In retrospect we can see that among the most significant of these was information regarding the research on atomic weapons.

Did Roosevelt appreciate that he had a proverbial ace up his sleeve with a potential new weapon of such destructive power that it would redefine the military balance? Did he withhold information regarding the atomic bomb in order to utilize it in future negotiations with the Soviets? Was he setting himself up to engage in serious diplomatic discussions in which the atomic bomb might be utilized as a bargaining chip? It seems unlikely.[24] For a start Roosevelt occasionally mused of advising the Soviets on the atomic secrets but simply never moved on the matter. On March 9, 1945, he told Canadian Prime Minister MacKenzie King that "he thought the Russians had been experimenting and knew something about what was being done. He thought the time had come to tell them how far the developments had gone. [But] Churchill was opposed to this."[25] The president greeted Secretary Stimson's recommendation for the exclusion of Russia on the grounds that "it was essential not to take them into our confidence until we were sure to get a real *quid pro quo* from our frankness" with tepid agreement rather than enthusiastic endorsement.[26]

Stimson clearly saw the future sharing of atomic information as a potential diplomatic tool, but it is striking to note that Roosevelt himself never spoke of it in this manner. For the most part he postponed decisions on the issue and held to the terms of the Hyde Park aide-memoire while awaiting the successful test of a weapon. In mid-March, Stimson "went

---

[24] For a different conclusion see Campbell Craig and Sergey Radchenko, *The Atomic Bombs and the Origins of the Cold War* (New Haven, CT, 2008), pp. 30–31. They argued that Roosevelt "sought to use the atomic project as a negotiating tool" against both the British and the Soviets.

[25] J. W. Pickersgill and D. F. Forster, eds., *The Mackenzie King Record*, Vol. II, 1944–1945 (Toronto, 1968), pp. 326–327.

[26] Stimson Diaries, Papers of Henry L. Stimson, Sterling Memorial Library, Yale University, New Haven, CT, December 31, 1944.

over with him the two schools of thought that exist in respect to the future control after the war of this project in case it is successful, one of them being the secret close-in attempted control of the project by those who control it now, and the other being the international control based upon freedom both of science and of access."[27] Stimson advised that the president must settle these matters before the first use of a bomb and FDR agreed but his death intervened before he made any firm decisions. In the end it was Truman who presided over the birth of the atomic age. When he did so he had some guidance that Roosevelt meant the new weapon to be used in the war against the Japanese, but little specific direction as to if and how the weapon should be subjected to international control and little indication that his predecessor planned to use it, in one way or another, as a weapon in his diplomatic arsenal.

As late as March 15, 1945, when Stimson met the president, he still felt obliged to defend the Manhattan Project against another of FDR's advisers who doubted its viability. Apparently James Clement (Jimmy) Dunn, a senior State Department official who directed the Office of European Affairs, had told FDR that he had been sold "a lemon" by his scientific advisers.[28] Stimson eagerly reassured Roosevelt to the contrary, and by this point the "gamble" of the immense endeavor to build an atomic bomb appeared likely to pay off. With the war in Europe entering its final months, the scientists had kept up their furious efforts even though they knew that the weapon they worked on would not be used to counter Hitler.

After various setbacks in the fall of 1944 it became clearer in the late winter of 1945 that bombs might be ready by the summer. Oppenheimer and his colleagues in a prodigious effort explored the two major possibilities – the first, using U-235, and, the second, plutonium. Different bomb designs eventually were required for each fuel. The original hope was "to use a so-called gun assembly, in which a critical mass is assembled by firing one segment of the fuel into a target made of the same material, thereby initiating the nuclear explosion." This design was dubbed the Thin Man, after a Dashiell Hammett novel, but it was eventually shortened for the U-235 bomb and became known as the Little Boy. The gun assembly proved unsuitable for the plutonium weapon so the Los Alamos scientists developed "a different arrangement, using shaped charges to implode or

---

[27] Stimson Diaries, March 15, 1945. Also see Hewlett and Anderson, *The New World*, pp. 333–340.
[28] Henry L. Stimson and McGeorge Bundy, *On Active Service in Peace and War* (New York, 1947), p. 615. Stimson Diaries, March 15, 1945.

squeeze a sphere of plutonium into a critical mass." They dubbed this device the Fat Man after the Sidney Greenstreet character in the recent movie *The Maltese Falcon*. The atomic bomb then, as Michael Gordin helpfully summarized, "came in two variants: Little Boy (uranium), easy to engineer as an explosive device, but very difficult to separate the fuel for; and Fat Man (plutonium), easier to generate fuel for, but posing a significant problem of engineering in the implosion mechanism."[29] It would not be until July 1945 that the implosion device would be tested. By that point Harry Truman had occupied the Oval office for almost three months.

[29] The direct quotations and the substance of this paragraph are from Michael Gordin, *Five Days in August: How World War II Became a Nuclear War* (Princeton, NJ, 2007), pp. 42–43.

CHAPTER 2

Harry Truman, Henry Stimson, and Atomic Briefings

Late in the afternoon of April 12, 1945, Presidential Press Secretary Steve Early summoned Harry Truman to the White House. Expecting to see President Franklin Roosevelt, he was ushered instead into the study of Eleanor Roosevelt. "Harry," she informed him, "the President is dead." Momentarily stunned, Truman eventually spoke and asked with genuine concern, "Is there anything I can do for you?" Mrs. Roosevelt replied insightfully: "Is there anything we can do for you for you are the one in trouble now." Within two hours Truman recited the oath of office, becoming the thirty-third president of the United States. Immediately after his swearing-in ceremony the new president addressed the hastily convened cabinet. "It was my intention," Truman recalled saying, "to continue both the foreign and domestic policies of the Roosevelt Administration."[1] He sincerely attempted to fulfill this pledge. Understanding how he did so, and appreciating the new president's basic convictions and his broad approach on foreign policy, are essential for apprehending the place that the atomic bomb played in his formulation of it.

Truman's comprehension of the details of Roosevelt's foreign policy and his grasp of the contemporary international situation were distinctly limited, to put it mildly. But it is important to appreciate that he was not some sort of human *tabula rasa* on these matters. His arrival in the United States Senate in 1935 forced him to devote some sustained – if, at times, naive – attention to defense and foreign policy questions. He eventually emerged as a forthright advocate of military preparedness in response to

---

[1] This account is taken mainly from Truman's memoir. See Harry S. Truman, *Memoirs*, Vol. 1, *Year of Decisions* (New York, 1955), pp. 15, 19.

fascist aggression in Europe and Asia and then, during the war, as an active proponent of American involvement in a postwar international organization specifically, and in world affairs generally.

Truman also possessed a special interest in military matters. He served in World War I, and this proved to be truly "the turning point in his life."[2] As Capt. Harry Truman he commanded Battery D of the 129th Field Artillery attached to the 35th Division. He saw some fierce and bloody action and participated in the Meuse-Argonne offensive of 1918. Across the Atlantic and far from home he discovered that he possessed courage under fire and that he could lead men. The latter discovery redirected his life, for leading men in war suggested to him the possibility of leading them in peacetime. His wartime contacts led directly to his political career and to his long association with the corrupt Pendergast machine in Kansas City throughout the 1920s. The Pendergast organization's votes also helped carry him to his eventual victory in the U.S. Senate race of 1934.

"The Senator from Pendergast" kept a low profile during his early years in Washington D.C., attending primarily to his domestically oriented committee work and suffering the snubs of many, including the White House, which took his solid support for the New Deal for granted. With the outbreak of World War II in September 1939 Truman emerged as a promoter of American military preparedness, and he supported major increases in American defense spending. After a tough but successful reelection battle in 1940, in which he proved his mettle and toughness as a politician, Truman returned to the Senate eager to contribute more in this crucial area.

In a thoughtful speech in the Senate early in 1941 the newly reelected senator outlined areas in the national defense program, especially in the letting of defense contracts, which demanded investigation. Having unsuccessfully volunteered for renewed military service, Truman wanted to ensure that expenditures were wisely spent as the United States moved to rebuild its defense forces – especially its army and army air corps – after allowing them to waste away to a mere skeletal operation during the 1930s. He secured the establishment of a special investigating committee to undertake the task, chaired it, and his energetic leadership of what became known as the Truman Committee in time "reconstructed his image from that of a machine politician to a statesman of democracy."[3] The terms of reference of Truman's committee limited the sphere of its

[2] David McCullough, *Truman* (New York, 1992), p. 102.
[3] Alonzo Hamby, *Man of the People: A Life of Harry S. Truman* (New York, 1995), p. 260.

investigation to the defense production program. It did not impinge on defense policy or strategy or on foreign policy, and Truman consciously attempted to avoid any moves that might leave his committee open to the charge of trying to "run defense."[4]

Senator Truman's work on his investigating committee brought about his first serious encounter with Secretary of War Henry L. Stimson. Truman and Stimson made a study in contrasts in their education, experience, and social standing, although the War Department head also had served as a U.S. Army artillery officer in France during World War I. Colonel Stimson epitomized the Waspish East Coast establishment of the time, which disdained the coarse machine politics transacted in Boss Tom Pendergast's Kansas City. Educated at Yale, where naturally he belonged to the Skull and Bones secret society, and at Harvard Law School, Stimson then joined a prestigious New York law firm headed by the future secretary of state, Elihu Root. His long career of public service began in 1906 when then President Theodore Roosevelt appointed him U.S. attorney for the southern district of New York. In 1910, he ran as the Republican candidate for governor of New York but his defeat soured him on the trials and tribulations of electoral politics although not on his high-minded public commitments. Over the next three decades his significant appointments included secretary of war during the Taft administration, governor-general of the Philippines under Coolidge, and secretary of state under Hoover's presidency, during which he issued his "Stimson Doctrine" of nonrecognition in response to Japanese aggression in Manchuria. Roosevelt tapped the firmly interventionist and now seventy-three-year-old Stimson in 1940 to return to the War Department to give a bipartisan flavor to his defense build-up. Stimson thereupon oversaw the rapid expansion of the U.S. Army to a force that would eventually number ten million soldiers.[5]

Explaining the gigantic American military expansion brought him before Truman's committee on April 15, 1941. Stimson undoubtedly looked upon Truman as a mere machine politician. His lack of regard for the Missouri senator can be inferred from his diary entry that portrayed the origins of the Senate Investigating Committee in Truman's desire to make "political capital and publicity" out of attacking the Army and the War Department as they grew quickly. Stimson prepared thoroughly for his meeting but found Truman and his colleagues to be "as mild as milk."

[4] Truman, *Year of Decisions*, pp. 190–191.
[5] See Godfrey Hodgson, *The Colonel: The Life and Wars of Henry L. Stimson, 1867–1950* (New York, 1990).

Quite relieved, he noted that there existed "no latent hostility in the air around me."[6] This placid encounter, however, did not serve to initiate any consequential relationship between the two men. Their quite different backgrounds meant that they moved in rather separate social circles, and Stimson suspiciously continued to think of Truman as just a self-interested politician. But this particular machine politician contributed constructively to the area where his Jackson County expertise could be applied – matters of contracts and construction of defense infrastructure – and he worked to make the United States more effective in the war he knew was coming for it.

The Japanese attack on Pearl Harbor finally brought the United States into the vast conflagration we know as World War II. It was barely two decades since Truman and his men had crossed the Atlantic to defeat the kaiser. Now an even stronger and more brutal German foe confronted them in Europe in alliance with a Japanese empire, which quickly dominated all of Asia. With the nation at war and committing its tremendous energies and resources to build a massive military force, the Missouri senator pursued his demanding work so vigorously that at times he suffered physical exhaustion. He toured defense plants regularly and issued reports that identified incompetence, bottlenecks, and wasteful spending. He worked well with both Republican and Democratic committee members and gained valuable experience in bipartisan cooperation. His labors attracted national attention. A survey of Washington newsmen conducted for the general-interest magazine *Look* in 1944 voted him as one of the ten most valuable officials in Washington, although Henry Stimson assuredly did not rank him so highly.

The inquiring probes of Truman's committee to investigate the national defense program brought about his initial brush with the Manhattan Project in June 1943. He had been alerted by Lewis Schwellenbach, a onetime colleague and the former senator from Washington, of the vast land purchases involving "some sort of DuPont project" along the Columbia River in the Hanford-Pasco–White Bluffs area of the state. Truman's initial inquiries about this acquisition of 200,000 acres of farmland apparently provoked a phone call from an edgy Stimson who alerted Truman that it "was part of a very important secret development" and persuaded him not to proceed with any further investigations. Truman quickly acceded to the request and told Stimson plainly that he could see "the situation" and that "you won't have to say another word to me."[7] He broadly kept this pledge, although he gleaned enough information to write

---

[6] Stimson Diaries, April 15, 1941. [7] Stimson Diaries, June 17, 1943.

to Schwellenbach on July 15 that the land was being used for "a plant to make a terrific explosion for a secret weapon that will be a wonder."[8] Later in the year one of the committee's investigators, Truman's old Kansas City friend Fred Canfil, even visited the Hanford area but was rebuffed firmly when he attempted to enter the defense department plant. He reported to Truman on his efforts but Truman didn't pursue the matter further at that point. Perhaps then one might say that Truman had some hint of the basic details of a huge secret project but hardly any firm grasp as to its purpose. Stimson kept it that way, and he assured that Truman remained largely ignorant of the development of the atomic bomb.

Continued concerns about the expenditures directed to the Manhattan Project brought Truman back into contact with Stimson in March 1944, much to Stimson's irritation. No doubt he had expected the senator to trust him like a true gentleman and not to trouble him again, but instead Truman questioned him forthrightly about whether the huge "Pasco Project" was being carried out "in a wasteful manner." Stimson replied on March 13 and again fended Truman off, while reminding him in a patronizing way of his earlier promise not to investigate the project. He assured his senate interrogator that the question of "waste cannot be justly or properly ascertained until the project has been carried out and its necessity and purpose understood." He also made it very clear that neither Truman nor any investigator from his staff would receive any briefing on the secret project. Later, Stimson's animosity toward the Missouri senator gushed forth onto the pages of his diary. He branded Truman "a nuisance and a pretty untrustworthy man, [who] talks smoothly but acts meanly."[9] Even after Truman became vice president Stimson didn't deign to brief him about the atomic bomb. Of course, what Truman didn't know hardly bothered him. Whatever his occasional delving at the very far edges of the Manhattan Project, he had other issues to attend to at the time.

In addition to his efforts regarding national defense, Truman poured considerable energy into the promotion of American entry into a new international organization and the defeat of isolationism. He wanted the United States to right the "wrong" of its refusal to ratify the Versailles Treaty and to participate in the League of Nations after World War I. The overblown rhetoric of this plain man suggests the depth of his convictions on the issue. "Do we not owe it our children, to all mankind," he asked of

---

[8] Truman to Schwellenbach, July 15, 1943, Harry S. Truman Papers, Harry S. Truman Library, Senatorial and Vice-Presidential Correspondence File, Box 231.

[9] Stimson Diaries, March 13, 1944.

an audience in Toledo in June 1944, "to be sure that these catastrophes do not engulf the world a third time. This is America's destiny."[10] Later in the year he wrapped the United States in a divine mantle and asserted that "Almighty God intends this nation to assume leadership in world affairs to preserve the peace."[11]

Such deep internationalist sentiments helped make Truman an acceptable compromise candidate for the vice presidency at the 1944 Democratic Party Convention. Truman had planned to nominate his onetime senate colleague James F. Byrnes for the position. Yet, after FDR conveyed to a hesitant Truman that "if he wants to break up the Democratic Party in the middle of a war that's his responsibility," the issue was sealed. The dutiful Truman gained release from his commitment to Byrnes and allowed his name to be placed in nomination against the sitting Vice President Henry Wallace. He won decisively on the second ballot.[12]

After his nomination Truman toured the country extensively hammering home a very partisan message, which equated support for the Republicans with isolationism. He warned against a "Congress of Nyes and Tafts," compared Thomas Dewey to Warren G. Harding, and challenged the Republican nominee to disassociate himself from eight isolationist senators in his party.[13] He met with Roosevelt infrequently during the campaign and received no substantial and specific briefings on policy matters. It is possible that he may have received from FDR some very vague details of the Manhattan Project, but the subject hardly registered with him.[14]

On January 20 the presidential inauguration took place on the south portico of the White House. Henry Wallace administered the oath to Truman, and then Roosevelt struggled to his feet and took the presidential oath for the fourth time. Just two days later the president left for Yalta in the Crimea to meet with Josef Stalin and Winston Churchill. Even upon his return from Yalta, Roosevelt gave Truman no serious briefings. Of course, it was hardly his way to share information freely and so, he feared, to weaken his control over policy making. Truman made no special effort to compensate for the presidential reticence. He assembled no policy-oriented

---

[10] Truman speech, Toledo, Ohio, June 14, 1944, Truman Papers, Senatorial and Vice-Presidential Speeches File.

[11] *New York Times*, October 25, 1944.

[12] Robert H. Ferrell is excellent on all the details. See his *Harry S. Truman: A Life* (Columbia, MO, 1994), pp. 165–171.

[13] *New York Times*, October 22, 24, 1944.

[14] On this matter see Ferrell, *Harry S. Truman*, p. 172.

staff as vice president and certainly had no influential foreign policy advisers. He sought neither briefings from the state and war departments nor consultations with American officials who had accompanied FDR to Yalta. A denial that the great leader could be struck down on the eve of victory beset Truman as it did everyone else in the administration. All those around the president "continued to play their private game of pushing mortality into the indefinite future."[15]

Roosevelt's disgraceful failure to brief his vice president fully only served to confirm Truman in his own foreign policy views that he found confirmed by the president's public statements. On his return from Yalta, FDR assured a joint session of the Congress that "the Crimean Conference was a successful effort by the three leading nations to find a common ground for peace ... it spells – and it ought to spell – the end of the system of unilateral action, exclusive alliances, and spheres of influence, and balances of power and all the other expedients which have been tried for centuries and failed."[16] A new day was dawning. Power politics would be dispatched to the dustbin of history. Truman joined the legislators on their feet applauding the president and the future peace he promised.

After a month in Washington upon his return from Yalta, Roosevelt left for his retreat in Warm Springs, intent on regaining his strength under the warm Georgia sun. Truman had little opportunity to deepen his relationship with the president during this time. He recalled that he saw Roosevelt only twice aside from at cabinet meetings where "Roosevelt never discussed anything important."[17] Then, on April 12, Franklin Roosevelt died. Within hours Harry Truman was sworn in as president and assumed the great responsibility for leading his nation through to victory in war and to success in formulating a lasting peace. He brought to the presidency a firm belief that a peaceful postwar world depended upon the adoption by the United States of world leadership in both the political and economic spheres. He saw the establishment and operation of a new world organization as crucial and viewed the meeting to design such a body, which was scheduled to meet in San Francisco late in April, as tremendously important. Like his predecessor he expected to work in collaboration with the wartime allies in shaping the postwar international

---

[15] Henry Morgenthau III, "The Last Night at Warm Springs," *New York Times*, December 4, 1995.

[16] *Congressional Record*, 91, Part 2, pp. 1621–1622.

[17] Truman mentioned this to Jonathan Daniels. See Jonathan Daniels, *The Man of Independence* (Philadelphia, 1950), p. 259. See also Truman, *Year of Decisions*, pp. 34–35.

structure. Truman certainly did not bring to the presidency any significant reservations concerning the policies or goals of Franklin Roosevelt as he understood them.

The Truman who took up the responsibilities of the presidential office in April 1945 possessed many of the fine qualities that his admirers delight in noting. He was indeed "a person of tough fiber, plain, warm manners, direct approach, and earthy humor," who possessed both courage and the capacity to make a decision.[18] But he was more complex than this. Truman also was, as David McCullough has observed, "unprepared, bewildered and frightened" as he put on the mantle of office.[19] He looked "strained but grim" as he took the presidential oath.[20] No doubt in his early days in office Truman must have been torn by inner doubts about his own abilities to fill the gigantic shoes into which he had stepped. He also must have been aware in a general sense of the suspicions of many both within and outside the administration that he simply was not up to the job. He might not have read TVA director David Lilienthal's description of him as "Throttlebottom Truman," or heard Navy Secretary James Forrestal murmuring after his swearing-in ceremony, "Poor little fellow, poor little fellow," but the low estimates of Truman pervaded the atmosphere.[21] Fearing to appear "indecisive and ignorant" and manfully aware that the country needed him to rise to the occasion, he accentuated his forcefulness and decisiveness.[22] Some mixture – the exact ingredients of which are not subject to historical analysis – of courage and inner strength as well as of bravado regarding his capacity to make decisions drove him forward through pressure-filled days.

Whatever his desire to convey decisiveness and to present an image of himself as in full control of his position, Truman never acted precipitously or erratically on major matters of policy. "Every major decision of his presidency," Alonzo Hamby insightfully has noted, "was the product of careful political or diplomatic planning and group consensus, not

---

[18] The quotation is from Robert J. Donovan, *Tumultuous Years: The Presidency of Harry S. Truman, 1949–1953* (New York, 1982), p. 395.

[19] McCullough, *Truman*, p. 355.

[20] The description of Truman is that of Joseph Davies in "Death of Roosevelt," April 12, 1945, Davies diary, Davies Papers, Library of Congress, Box 16.

[21] David E. Lilienthal, *The Journals of David E. Lilienthal*, Vol. 1, *The TVA Years, 1939–1945* (New York, 1964), p. 690; and Forrestal quoted in Townsend Hoopes and Douglas Brinkley, *Driven Patriot: The Life and Times of James Forrestal* (New York, 1992), pp. 204–205.

[22] My thinking here is influenced some by Ronald Steel, "Harry of Sunnybrook Farm," *The New Republic* (August 10, 1992), p. 37.

individual whim." This decision-making approach was evident from Truman's earliest days and would be evident in his decision making regarding the use of the atomic bomb. "The man who liked to present himself as a quick decision maker was actually slow and cautious on the big things."[23] From his first hours in office Truman relied on advisers much more than did Roosevelt. And these advisers (and events themselves) tended to frame the issues for him to decide and determine the timing of them. Only rarely did Truman personally frame the issue or set the agenda and he came to the presidency with no desire whatsoever to forge any major new direction in policy.

On that traumatic first evening as president, Truman requested that all cabinet members remain in their posts. He asked for their support and promised, as Secretary of State Edward Stettinius recalled, "that he would carry on to the best of his ability."[24] At the close of Truman's first cabinet meeting, Secretary Stimson claimed his attention and informed the new commander in chief of "an immense project that was underway – a project looking to the development of a new explosive of almost unbelievable power."[25] Such a cryptic summary constituted Stimson's first briefing, however limited, for Truman concerning the Manhattan Project to develop the atomic bomb. Now the secretary of war felt compelled to enlighten the president of progress on building an atomic bomb, but his audience of one seemed less than interested. There is no evidence that Truman made any immediate connection between this project and the one he had been warned off in 1943. Presumably with his head spinning from the speed and weight of events, he asked no questions of Stimson. Certainly he gained neither a full appreciation nor any real understanding of the potential of this new weapon. Later that evening Truman released a statement to counter enemy propaganda, which assured the world "that we will prosecute the war on both fronts, east and west, with all the vigor we possess to a successful conclusion."[26] He had no sense yet that the weapon Stimson mentioned would play a key role in fulfilling this promise.

On his first full day in office Truman received a series of briefings to familiarize himself with the foreign and defense policies for which he now

---

[23] Alonzo L. Hamby, "An American Democrat: A Reevaluation of the Personality of Harry S. Truman," *Political Science Quarterly*, Vol. 106 (Spring, 1991), p. 52.

[24] Record, April 12, 1945, Edward R. Stettinius, Jr. Papers, Alderman Library, University of Virginia, Box 224.

[25] Truman, *Year of Decisions*, p. 20.

[26] Truman's statement, April 12, 1945, *Public Papers of the Presidents of the United States: Harry S. Truman, 1945* (Washington, D.C., 1961), p. 1.

bore responsibility. He met with the military leaders of the United States – Secretary Stimson and Secretary of the Navy Forrestal, Gen. George C. Marshall and two admirals, Ernest J. King and William D. Leahy. They provided him with a pointed report on the efforts of the Allies on all fronts and gave estimates concerning the defeat of Germany and Japan. The Nazis, they cautiously predicted, would be defeated within six months but a Japanese surrender could not be expected for at least eighteen months.[27] Soviet forces in the East and the Anglo-American forces in the West were rapidly closing their huge vise on Germany and were within two weeks of meeting each other at the Elbe River at Torgau. With air superiority established the western forces advanced on a broad front, taking the surrender of hundreds of thousands of Germans as they marched forward. Yet, the chiefs of staff focused the new president's attention less on the likelihood of an imminent German collapse but on the possibility of Hitler's making a last stand in a mountain redoubt in the south of his battered nation.

The situation in the Pacific war remained extremely challenging. Although the U.S. Navy now enforced a blockade on Japan and American B-29s under the command of General Curtis LeMay pounded its cities, the Japanese continued their ferocious resistance and inflicted high casualties on the U.S. forces in a furious effort to defend the remaining outposts protecting their home islands. The battle for Okinawa, in the Ryukyu island chain and within easy flying distance of Kyushu, had begun just days before FDR's death and would grind on with appalling losses until mid-June. Extrapolating that the Japanese troops would defend their home islands with comparable ferocity, the chiefs' estimate of eighteen months seemed reasonable.

Truman accepted the reports of his military advisers without question. He made no pretense to being a military strategist. He neither probed his advisers about broad strategy nor the tactics being applied in specific military theaters. He simply wanted them to continue moving forward to defeat the Nazis and the Japanese militarists as they had done for his predecessor. This meeting clarified that there would be essential continuity between Roosevelt and Truman in the military domain. Further confirming the point was Truman's seizing the opportunity as the meeting broke up to request that Admiral Leahy stay on in his position as chief of staff to the president. The tough-minded and flinty old sailor agreed and he continued to be closely involved in American military and diplomatic decision making.

---

[27] On this meeting see Truman, *Year of Decisions*, p. 29.

The new president's clear recognition of his limitations in the foreign policy domain prompted him to seek briefings and assistance from those whom he thought possessed greater knowledge of Roosevelt's plans. Foremost among those whose aid he sought stood the man he had planned to nominate for vice president in 1944, James F. Byrnes. Byrnes had hurried back to Washington from his home in Spartanburg, South Carolina at Truman's request, and came to see the president during the afternoon of April 13. "Understandably," Byrnes later wrote with just a hint of condescension, "he was overwhelmed by the task that had devolved so suddenly on him and was trying to familiarize himself with the more urgent problems confronting him."[28] Truman took the opportunity to question Byrnes about the Yalta conference proceedings. His approach was that of one determined to learn more of the agreements that Roosevelt had negotiated and the policies he intended to pursue.

Byrnes, however, used the occasion to brief Truman further on the Manhattan Project with which he was familiar from his work as director of the Office of War Mobilization during 1942–1944. He emphasized the vast investment of materials and funds in the project and the potential power of the weapon it aimed to produce.[29] The subject undoubtedly registered with the new president, but at this meeting Truman was more concerned to introduce to Byrnes his desire for the former senator to play a prominent part in the new administration, indeed possibly for him to serve as secretary of state. Truman's awareness that the secretary of state stood next in the line of succession to the presidency – as was constitutional practice prior to the ratification of the Twenty-Fifth Amendment in 1967 – convinced him that someone who had served in elective office should hold the job. Byrnes eventually would take over the State Department in early July 1945, and as both secretary of state and as an informal adviser beforehand Byrnes proved to be a key Truman counselor on atomic issues.

Issues concerning the atomic bomb assuredly were not at the forefront of Truman's concerns during his early days in office. Facilitating a successful meeting of the allied powers at San Francisco to establish the United Nations was the principal foreign policy concern Truman faced. He also confronted the tension that now existed in U.S.-Soviet relations over such issues as the composition of the Polish government, the failures in

---

[28] James F. Byrnes, *All in One Lifetime* (New York, 1958), p. 280.
[29] On Byrnes briefing Truman on the A-bomb see David Robertson, *Sly and Able: A Political Biography of James F. Byrnes* (New York, 1994), pp. 390–391.

establishing the Allied Control Commissions in Bulgaria, Rumania, and Hungary, occupation policy for Germany, the surrender procedure and zones of occupation in Germany, policy for the occupation of Austria, the Yugoslav threat to Trieste, and the possible admission of Argentina to the San Francisco meeting. He surely must have staggered a little at the number and complexity of the problems that confronted him.

Truman's concern to resolve the issue concerning the composition of the Polish government led to his initial meeting with Soviet Foreign Minister Viacheslav Molotov on April 22, 1945, and to a much sharper exchange the following day. The latter meeting has been used to justify such dramatically tempting hypotheses as that of a "sudden reversal" by Truman of Roosevelt's conciliatory approach to the Soviet Union, and as reflecting his decision to force an "immediate showdown" with the Soviets.[30] But Truman's more forceful approach at the April 23 meeting owed to his hopes to break the impasse on the Polish issue and thereby to guarantee a successful meeting at San Francisco. Truman saw himself as working to uphold Roosevelt's agreements. His earnest desire to continue his predecessor's policies stayed with him in the weeks and months ahead and it certainly characterized his approach on the atomic bomb.

In dealing with the range of challenging issues that he faced, Truman remained heavily dependent on his advisers. Initially there was no dominant voice among them. Truman took counsel from a number of different officials and tended to consider a variety of issues in quite discrete terms. No person or agency effectively considered how American military strategy, economic power, and atomic potential might serve the diplomacy of the nation. Truman merely muddled through like some struggling student learning in pressured circumstances from a group of competing professors who based their respective instruction on differing assumptions and assessments of the situation at hand. Surprisingly, in light of later suggestions of his abandonment of FDR's cooperative approach, he increasingly accepted the views of those counselors who advocated a less confrontational approach toward the Soviet Union than the one he demonstrated in his meeting with Molotov.

While differences over a range of issues simmered as the war in Europe entered its final weeks, diplomats from allied and associated countries labored in San Francisco to forge a new international peacekeeping

---

[30] For "sudden reversal" see Denna Frank Fleming, *The Cold War and Its Origins, 1917–1960* (Garden City, NY, 1961), pp. 265–270. For "immediate showdown" see Gar Alperovitz, *Atomic Diplomacy*, rev. ed., (New York, 1985), pp. 19–40.

body. Truman opened the conference with a radio address on April 25 when he put before the assembled delegates a choice between "the continuance of international chaos – or the establishment of a world organization for the enforcement of peace." He asked them to create the structure "which will make future peace, not only possible, but certain."[31] He held to this rather utopian goal with deep conviction.

On the same day that Truman held forth on his vision for a new world peacekeeping organization, Stimson eagerly sought to instruct the president on the implications of the potentially devastating new weapon being developed by the Manhattan Project. Only then did he and General Leslie Groves, the project director, get the opportunity to give Truman a lengthy briefing on the atomic bomb.[32] Groves reported on the genesis and current status of the atomic project while Stimson spoke to a memorandum explaining the implications of the bomb for international relations. He addressed the potential terrifying power of the new weapon, advising that "within four months, we shall in all probability have completed the most terrible weapon ever known in human history, one bomb of which could destroy a whole city." He went on to allude to the dangers that its discovery and development foreshadowed, and pointed to the difficulty in constructing a realistic system of controls. He then suggested that "the question of sharing it with other nations and, if so shared, upon what terms, becomes a primary question of our foreign relations."[33]

Stimson's briefing on April 25 alerted Truman to the relationship, or more accurately the potential relationship, between the atomic bomb and American policy toward the Soviet Union, but the president did not appear to have paid due attention to the lesson. Certainly he did not share Stimson's virtual obsession with the matter.[34] It seems that Truman focused less on the geopolitical implications of the possession of the atomic bomb and more on the personal burden of his having to authorize the use of an awesome weapon. "I am going to have to make a decision which no man in history has ever had to make," he reportedly said to White House staffer Leonard Reinsch, the very next person he saw after Stimson and Groves left his office. "I'll make the decision, but it is terrifying to think

---

[31] Truman address to the United Nations Conference, April 25, 1945, *Public Papers of the Presidents: Harry S. Truman*, 1945 (Washington, D.C., 1961), p. 21.

[32] Truman, *Year of Decisions*, p. 104.   [33] Stimson Diaries, April 25, 1945.

[34] On Stimson see Stimson and Bundy, *On Active Service in Peace and War*, pp. 612–633; McGeorge Bundy, *Danger and Survival: Choices About the Bomb in the First Fifty Years* (New York, 1988), pp. 54–129; and Sean Malloy, *Atomic Tragedy: Henry L. Stimson and the Decision to Use the Bomb Against Japan* (Ithaca, NY, 2008).

about what I will have to decide."[35] Truman's sober contemplation of the possibility of authorizing the use of a weapon that might destroy a whole city, however, did not prompt his detailed reflection concerning the potential impact of the new weapon for international relations in general or his dealings with the Soviets in particular. Gar Alperovitz's elaborate and fanciful constructions to the contrary, he did not begin to design American diplomacy toward the Soviet Union in light of the impending possession of the atomic bomb.[36] Suggestions that he adopted some strategy of "delayed showdown" in which he deliberately chose to defer consideration of major issues with the Soviets until he held this weapon in the American arsenal impute a coherence to his foreign policy formulation that simply did not exist. Truman's unwillingness to build his foreign policy upon the potential of an as yet untested weapon received further ballast from the skeptical views of Admiral Leahy regarding the potential of the atomic bomb. The old sailor described it as "the biggest fool thing we have ever done. The bomb will never go off, and I speak as an expert in explosives."[37]

Following another meeting with Stimson on May 2 Truman appointed an advisory group, the Interim Committee, to consider the various questions raised by the anticipated success in developing an atomic weapon. He appointed Stimson as chair and designated James Byrnes to serve on it as his personal representative. The other members included George L. Harrison, Stimson's key aide on atomic matters; Ralph A. Bard, undersecretary of the navy; William L. Clayton, assistant secretary of state; Dr. Vannevar Bush, director, Office of Scientific Research and Development; Dr. Karl T. Compton, chief of the Office of Field Service in Office of Scientific Research and Development; and Dr. James B. Conant, chairman of the National Defense Research Committee. These were serious and very experienced officials. Interestingly, Truman named Byrnes only upon Stimson's recommendation and had seemed quite willing to allow this body to undertake its work without his appointing a

[35] J. Leonard Reinsch oral history interview quoted in S. David Broscious, "Longing for International Control, Banking on American Superiority: Harry S. Truman's Approach to Nuclear Weapons," in John Lewis Gaddis, Philip H. Gordon, Ernest R. May, and Jonathan Rosenberg, eds., *Cold War Statesmen Confront the Bomb: Nuclear Diplomacy since 1945* (Oxford and New York, 1999), p. 16.

[36] Gar Alperovitz titled a chapter in his *Atomic Diplomacy* "The Decision to Postpone a Confrontation with Stalin," and developed elaborate details of a supposed "strategy of delay." See, *Atomic Diplomacy*, pp. 110–174.

[37] See Truman, *Year of Decisions*, p. 21.

specific delegate. The wily old war secretary, who undoubtedly had heard the rumors that Byrnes would replace Stettinius, presumably requested the South Carolinian to join the committee so as to gain him as an eventual conduit to the president, perhaps someone who might tutor the new chief executive on these matters.

Certainly Byrnes and Truman engaged in no prolonged discussion about his service on the Interim Committee. On May 3 Byrnes alerted his trusted friend Ben Cohen that he had been asked by Truman "to represent him on a Committee appointed by the Secretary of War to make an investigation of a matter so secret that he would not mention it over the telephone." Byrnes correctly suspected it had "to do with some of Vannevar Bush's work" and that it would involve him working with Stimson in the latter part of May.[38] As far as the written record reveals, Truman essentially left the committee to its own devices. The group focused more during May on questions regarding *how* the atomic bomb would be used against Japan – its use was simply assumed – than on its potential as a diplomatic lever for use in future negotiations with the Russians.[39] Certainly, Truman wasn't much influenced in his policy making toward the Soviet Union during May 1945 by the prospect of his nation's solitary possession of atomic weapons. While the redoubtable Stimson saw the two issues as crucially connected and spoke of the atomic bomb as potentially a "master card" in diplomacy, the elderly gentleman did not serve as Truman's close tutor in this area.[40] Truman respected Stimson but there was no simpatico or good chemistry between them and only the most formal of relationships. Stimson's diary reflections reveal that he was less than certain of the president's plans and perturbed that he was not pursuing a strategy that held the atomic bomb's potential as an important factor in his diplomacy. As if to confirm Stimson's anxieties, Truman did not track the deliberations of the Interim Committee with any

---

[38] Byrnes to Cohen, May 3, 1945, James F. Byrnes Papers, Cooper Library, Clemson University, Folder 189.

[39] For details on the early meetings of the Interim Committee see Hewlett and Anderson, *The New World*, pp. 353–354. Also note that Stimson later admitted that "the first and greatest problem was the decision on the use of the bomb." Stimson and Bundy, *On Active Service in Peace and War*, p. 617. Similarly, Byrnes remembered that the Committee's "primary and immediate function was to make recommendations on the preparations of a test explosion in New Mexico and, if this proved successful, on the use of the bomb against Japan." James F. Byrnes, *All in One Lifetime*, p. 283.

[40] Stimson Diaries, May 15, 1945. Stimson diary reflections reveal that he was less than certain of the president's plans and perturbed that he was not conscientiously and clearly pursuing a strategy which saw the atomic bomb as a "master card."

care and simply waited for it to present conclusions to him. He had many more pressing matters to occupy his attention such as overseeing the final defeat of Nazi Germany.

Ending the war in Europe forced Truman to engage in a pointed argument with the British prime minister over the use of military forces for political ends. Churchill objected to General Dwight D. Eisenhower's decision to stop his military advance at the Elbe. The British leader wanted the Anglo-American forces to capture both Berlin and Prague if possible. He obviously saw the political value of such military successes. The prime minister first tried to prod Eisenhower but without success. The supreme allied commander, seemingly paying little attention to Carl Von Clausewitz's *On War*, refused "to intermingle political and military considerations."[41] Churchill thereupon tried an end-run around Eisenhower and appealed directly to Truman on April 30 arguing for the liberation of Prague and western Czechoslovakia. One might have expected his entreaty to have some impact on a president who had decided to alter Roosevelt's accommodating policy toward the Soviets. But Truman was not such a president. He did not seize this opportunity to use military forces for political ends. On the advice of General George Marshall, who bluntly noted that he "would be loath to hazard American lives for purely political purposes," Truman rejected Churchill's suggestion.[42] Also, as the military historian D. M. Giangreco recently has revealed well, both Marshall and Eisenhower worried that getting bogged down in any battle for Berlin or Prague would upset the carefully laid plans to redeploy American soldiers from the European theater to the Pacific to assist in an onerous invasion of the Japanese home islands.[43] This episode thus revealed not only Truman's general approach on military questions and his dependence on the advice of his key military advisers, but also that those advisers already thought far beyond the defeat of the Nazis to the demands of vanquishing the Japanese militarists.

During May and June of 1945 Truman also resisted the impassioned efforts of Winston Churchill to enlist him into a more firm approach with the Soviet Union. Churchill wanted to stand up to the Soviet domination of

---

[41] On Eisenhower's position see his message to Marshall, April 23, 1945, in Alfred D. Chandler, ed. *The Papers of Dwight David Eisenhower: The War Years* (Baltimore, 1970), p. 2583.

[42] Truman to Churchill, May 1, 1945, *FRUS 1945*, IV, p. 446. Marshall quoted in John Lewis Gaddis, *The United States and the Origins of the Cold War 1941–1947* (New York, 1972), p. 209.

[43] D. M. Giangreco, *Hell to Pay: Operation Downfall and the Invasion of Japan, 1945–1947* (Annapolis, MD, 2009), pp. 49–52.

Eastern Europe, already taking form in Poland and beyond. Truman, however, bore no desire to force or precipitate any conflict or confrontation with the Soviets. He wanted divisive issues settled and he desired to obtain Soviet cooperation generally in the postwar world order and, of course, the specific assistance of Stalin and his armies in the Pacific War. Truman and his advisers like former ambassador to Moscow Joseph Davies and Admiral Leahy feared that Churchill's actions would endanger the unity of the "Big Three" and the prospects for permanent peace.

In late May the president dispatched Harry Hopkins, FDR's closest aide, to Moscow, precisely to settle outstanding issues with Stalin and to finalize details for a summit meeting of the Big Three leaders. This mission displayed, as the diplomat Charles Bohlen later observed, "that the United States was prepared to go to considerable lengths to preserve friendship with the Soviet Union."[44] The mission and Truman's positive reaction toward it should lay to rest once and for all suggestions that the president was not genuinely seeking cooperation with Moscow. His eagerness to improve relations with Stalin led him to agree to a significant amelioration of the American stance on Poland as articulated in April. Like his predecessor he chose not to force the issue of Polish political independence and national sovereignty at a cost to amicable U.S.-Soviet relations.

In the weeks from the conclusion of Hopkins's mission until Truman's departure for the Potsdam Conference in July the United States approached a series of issues involving the Soviet Union in a businesslike and largely conciliatory manner. Naturally there remained substantial matters of disagreement but these came to be seen within a framework of continued Soviet-American friendship. Truman himself gave expression to these sentiments in diary reflections on June 7 where he reacted against anti-Soviet remarks made by Senator Burton Wheeler by noting that "every time we get things going halfway right with the Soviets some smart aleck has to attack them. If it isn't Willie Hearst, Bertie McCormick or Burt Wheeler it is some other bird who wanted to appease Germany but just can't see any good in Russia." While assuring himself that he was "not afraid of Russia," he tellingly noted that "they've always been our friends and I can't see any reason why they shouldn't always be so."[45]

The Americans consciously avoided giving any grounds for suspicion that they and the British were "ganging up" on their Slavic ally. This

---

[44] Charles E. Bohlen, *Witness to History, 1929–1969* (New York, 1973), p. 223.
[45] Diary entry, June 7, 1945, in Robert H. Ferrell, ed., *Off the Record: The Private Papers of Harry S. Truman* (New York, 1980), pp. 44–45.

sentiment lay behind Truman's refusal to meet with Churchill prior to the Potsdam meeting. It also caused the American joint chiefs of staff to reject the suggestion of their British counterparts that they meet in London prior to the Big Three heads of state meeting in Germany. In contrast to Churchill's increasingly dire assessment of the international situation regarding the Soviet Union, Truman held that differences were being resolved or set on the road to resolution. And this characterized the situation not only in Europe but also in Asia. In the Far East the compelling need to maintain momentum in the war against the Japanese guided American actions. The desire to gain Soviet participation in the Pacific conflict remained strong and guaranteed that Truman would move to facilitate the implementation of the Yalta Far Eastern Accord once Stalin had confirmed to Hopkins his commitment to enter the war in August.

When some word of the Yalta terms reached the Chinese in June, Chiang Kai-shek's foreign minister, T. V. Soong, hurried from the U.N. meeting in San Francisco to Washington. There, Truman explained the detailed terms of the Yalta accords to him and made very clear his strong commitment to the agreement reached by President Roosevelt.[46] Not surprisingly, Soong feared that Stalin had extracted a very high price at Chinese expense for his commitment to enter the war. The president turned to Joseph Davies, who now served as a key adviser, to convey to the Chinese official that the price needed to be paid, and this he coolly did. When Truman himself held a further meeting with the Chinese foreign minister on June 14 he hardly overflowed with empathy when Soong expressed concern about the Soviet demand for the Manchurian concessions. He promised to "do nothing which would harm the interests of China," but clarified that "his chief interest now was to see the Soviet Union participate in the Far Eastern War in sufficient time to be of help in shortening the war and thus save American and Chinese lives." In a revealing comment that captured well his attitude at this time, Truman added that "the United States desired above all to see these postwar questions settled in a way as to eliminate any tinderboxes both in Europe and in the Far East which might cause future trouble or wars."[47] So briefed in Washington, Soong soon departed for Moscow in a bid to clarify and agree on the details of the accord. The Soong-Stalin talks were still in progress when the American delegation departed for the Big Three conference, but from Truman's perspective he had acted appropriately to fulfill

---

[46] Grew memorandum of Truman-Soong conversation, June 9, 1945, *FRUS 1945*, VII, p. 896.
[47] Grew memorandum, June 14, 1945, *FRUS 1945*, VII, pp. 901–903.

FDR's Yalta pledges designed to gain Soviet participation in the costly war against the ferocious Japanese foe whose tenacity had led to such high casualties on Iwo Jima and Okinawa.

Before departing for Potsdam the president also played his part in bringing to fruition the effort to create the United Nations Organization. On June 25 he flew to San Francisco and enjoyed a ticker-tape reception on his journey downtown to the Fairmont Hotel. The next day he watched proudly as Secretary of State Stettinius signed the United Nations Charter for the United States and then the president addressed the delegates from fifty nations assembled in the opera house for their final session. "The Charter of the United Nations which you have just signed," he declared, "is a solid structure upon which we can build a better world." As befit his sincere internationalist sentiments his words were deeply felt and he hoped that they marked a historic day. The united spirit of the Allies, which had inspired them to defeat Fascism, must continue and the "powerful nations [must] assume the responsibility for leadership towards a world peace." Calling upon the memories of Woodrow Wilson and Franklin Roosevelt he called on the representatives "to grasp this supreme chance to establish a world-wide rule of reason – to create an enduring peace under the guidance of God."[48] Truman's lofty rhetoric aimed to match the grand occasion and reflected the high hopes and, it also must be said, the inflated and unreal expectations, which many Americans held for the United Nations.

Back in Washington, Truman personally delivered the Charter of the United Nations to the Senate of the United States. The chamber and galleries were filled to capacity as the president moved up the central aisle of the legislative body he loved so much. Behind him came his military aide, Brig. Gen. Harry H. Vaughan, carrying the blue-bound charter. Loud applause erupted when Truman handed it up to Senator Kenneth McKellar, president pro-tempore of the Senate, placing it at the mercy of his one-time colleagues. The president spoke briefly but forcefully and called on the Senate to ratify the treaty quickly. In subsequent hearings of the foreign relations committee the treaty met with wide approval and before the month was out the Senate ratified the U.N. treaty by a vote of eighty-nine to two. Even a political genius like Franklin Roosevelt could hardly have done better.

During a stopover in his hometown of Independence, Missouri, on his return journey from San Francisco, Truman held a press conference at

---

[48] Address at the Closing Session of the United Nations Conference, June 26, 1945, *Public Papers of Harry S. Truman, 1945*, pp. 138–139.

which he announced Edward Stettinius's resignation as secretary of state and his nomination as the first American representative to the United Nations. Shortly thereafter he confirmed what all political insiders already knew, that James F. Byrnes would be nominated to run the State Department. Truman wanted the South Carolinian, whose negotiating skills he so admired and with whom he felt at ease, to be at his side at Potsdam. The Byrnes nomination sailed through the Senate by unanimous vote on the same day that Truman delivered the U.N. charter. Truman's foreign policy now moved to a new stage in which the newly appointed secretary of state would prove a major figure including on the related issues of using the atomic bomb and forcing Japan's surrender.

Those who seek to understand Truman's thinking during the early months of his presidency must appreciate the sincerity of his hopes and expectations for good relations with the Soviet Union. Some years after he left the presidency, Truman expressed regret that Dean Acheson had not been with him at Potsdam rather than Jimmy Byrnes and Joseph Davies. In the midst of his musings about what might have been he described Davies as "a Russophile" and then added notably "as most of us were."[49] Unquestionably he put himself in this Russophile category and with some good reason. He had pursued the essentials of Roosevelt's policy designed to guarantee the collaboration of the major powers as the bedrock of a stable and peaceful postwar world order. He believed such an order to be possible and was rather naively unaware that Stalin was reading from a completely different script in terms of his postwar vision. In pursuing his broad foreign policy goals the prospect of possessing an atomic bomb had played no major role. Truman's attention to this weapon centered instead on what it might contribute to defeating Japan and ending the war in the Pacific.

---

[49] Truman to Acheson, March 15, 1957, Truman Papers, Post-Presidential Files, Box 44.

CHAPTER 3

James F. Byrnes, the Atomic Bomb, and the Pacific War

A proper accounting of the development of American policy to defeat Japan and bring World War II to an end must take due note of the crucial role played by James F. Byrnes. Although he is not well remembered today, the experienced South Carolinian possessed tremendous gifts for politics. His insightful biographer rightly titled his study *Sly and Able*. Comparing FDR and Byrnes, David Robertson asserted with some justification that "Roosevelt publicly outshone Byrnes at making friends; but behind the scenes Jimmy Byrnes was the better politician, and he knew it."[1] By the time he took command at the state department he had held a number of positions any one of which might have served others as the culmination of a fine career – senate majority leader, Supreme Court justice, and director of the Office of War Mobilization and Reconversion (OWMR), where his tremendous work running the home front earned him the sobriquet of "assistant president." Byrnes reacted to the disappointment of being passed over as FDR's running mate in 1944 with outward calm and true professionalism. His self-confidence and high regard for his own capacities were in no way damaged. He continued his important work at OWMR and spoke in support of the Roosevelt-Truman ticket. Perhaps he hoped that FDR would select him to succeed his good friend Cordell Hull at the state department, but the president judged Byrnes too independent for that task and picked the more malleable Edward Stettinius. Despite being passed over yet again this ambitious politician accepted Roosevelt's invitation to accompany him to Yalta. Subsequently, he used his considerable talents to sell the Yalta agreements to Congress and the American public.

---

[1] David Robertson, *Sly and Able*, p. 6.

Even though he then retired from OWMR, Byrnes continued to publicly and privately identify himself with Franklin Roosevelt's foreign policy approach.

Byrnes's journey with Roosevelt to the Crimea hardly transformed him into a foreign policy expert. Despite his presence in the Yalta conference room he was not particularly well versed in the details of foreign policy nor did he possess any significant international experience. Foreign policy issues had never been of primary concern for him. Domestic politics and policies always held the central claim on his attention and efforts. As secretary of state his concern about the domestic political consequences of international initiatives would influence strongly their nature and content. Of course, Truman and Byrnes held this in common. An astute British observer at the time rightly commented that Truman, "like Mr. Byrnes, [has] an outlook to some extent limited by concern with the home scene of the United States."[2] Indeed to understand the policies forged and pursued by the Truman-Byrnes partnership one must appreciate that these men were at heart capable politicians rather than international strategists. Truman's selection of Byrnes as his secretary of state owed largely to political concerns, and to Truman's confidence in and regard for his former Senate majority leader's abilities. It certainly did not indicate any desire to take foreign policy in a new direction. Neither Truman nor Byrnes had any well-developed notion in April–May of 1945 what such a direction might be. While Byrnes eventually availed himself of opportunities to learn the details of foreign policy developments he avoided offering any substantive recommendations on such matters prior to his taking office. His political savvy guided him to avoid giving cause for accusations that he was interfering with or undercutting Stettinius's efforts, and so to bide his time at home in Spartanburg, South Carolina.

There was but one major issue from Truman's swearing-in until the eve of Potsdam on which Byrnes exercised real impact on policy. His membership on the Interim Committee allowed him to influence American policy on the use of the atomic bomb. Through his work at OWMR Byrnes had developed some personal and political investment in the work of the Manhattan Project and a desire to justify the more than two billion dollars expended on it by 1945.[3] He had put this view firmly to Roosevelt in late

---

[2] This is the assessment of General Sir Gordon Macready, Head of the British Army Mission in Washington. See, Annex III to Orme Sargent, "Stocktaking after VE Day," in Prime Minister's Confidential File (Premier 4), Public Record Office [British Archives], File 31, Folder 5.

[3] For details see Robertson, *Sly and Able*, pp. 392–393.

1944 and early 1945. He even warned FDR in a memorandum on March 3, 1945, that "if the project proves a failure, it will then be subjected to relentless investigation and criticism," and recommended an impartial review of the project's progress.[4] Now he found himself strategically located to act upon it as the "president's personal representative" on the Interim Committee.

While Henry Stimson chaired this impressive committee, Byrnes exercised notable influence within it during the series of meetings held from May 9 to June 1. He blocked any moves aimed at a sharing of atomic research with the Soviets or even the British. That smacked of a giveaway and would be "politically untenable in Congress," and his view of the tenability of any measure in the congress proved difficult to dispute.[5] More significantly, at the end of May he lowered the boom on suggestions that either "the United States not use the atomic bomb on Japan or that it warn Japan before the bomb's use."[6] Leo Szilard, the physicist who had prompted Einstein to first raise the atomic bomb issue to Roosevelt, put such views directly before Byrnes when he and two colleagues, Harold Urey and Walter Bartky, traveled to Byrnes's home in Spartanburg on May 28, but they made no headway whatsoever. In discussing the politics of using the atomic bomb, Byrnes's biographer rightly has noted, the scientist and the future secretary of state "had not even spoken the same language." Szilard worried about the impact on relations with the Soviet Union, but as Robertson persuasively argues, for Byrnes "domestic political concerns were primary." Congress would want a return on the national investment in the Manhattan Project to be sure, but more importantly Byrnes believed that "both the public and their representatives would be outraged if the Truman administration later were shown to have displayed any reluctance to win the war with Japan as quickly as possible by forgoing the use of this weapon."[7] Perhaps he also hoped that the new weapon might have some beneficial diplomatic dividend in U.S. relations with the Soviet Union, although that could hardly be relied upon. One must note that other scientists also expressed reservations about the possibility that the atomic bomb would be used, most notably the group at the Metallurgical Laboratory at the University of Chicago headed by James Franck, but their representations had little impact.[8]

---

[4] Memorandum for the president, March 3, 1945, Byrnes Papers, Folder 596–2.
[5] Robertson, *Sly and Able*, p. 398.   [6] Robertson, *Sly and Able*, p. 399.
[7] Robertson, *Sly and Able*, p. 405.
[8] See Rotter, *Hiroshima: The World's Bomb*, pp. 149–151.

The use of the atomic bomb at Hiroshima is an event seared into the world's psyche. The mere mention of "Hiroshima" fuels the imagination with images of vast death and destruction on a scale never seen before. Yet it is crucial to recall that members of the Interim Committee never acted with that ghastly vision before them. Their minds were troubled more by the horrors of the Pacific War as seen through an American lens. The treachery of Pearl Harbor, the reports of Japanese atrocities, the suicidal resistance of the Japanese military at Iwo Jima and Okinawa stoked a deep antipathy to the Japanese Empire.[9] Little reserve of either respect or sympathy remained for the Japanese military and people who were viewed increasingly in a stereotyped racist manner.[10] The task at hand centered on defeating this ferocious foe as quickly as possible.

The Interim Committee held lengthy and important meetings on May 31 and June 1 during which they consulted with their Scientific Advisory panel and with representatives of the great industrial firms (Westinghouse, DuPont, and Union Carbide), which helped in the manufacture of the atomic bombs. They also drew on the counsel of the War Department's Target Committee, which recommended actions to shock the Japanese leaders and their people with the expected fearful power of these weapons.[11] The historian Sean Malloy rightly has noted that the work at Los Alamos "resulted in a weapon optimized for the destruction of cities and the killing of civilians."[12] This narrowed the options for policy makers but it led to no hesitations regarding the use of the weapons. On June 1 the committee formalized its crucial decisions under Byrnes's forceful guidance. The consensus held that the bomb be used against Japan as soon as possible, that it be used on "a vital war plant employing a large number of workers and closely surrounded by workers' houses," and that it be used without prior warning.[13]

The Interim Committee left much of the detailed planning for the actual use of the bombs in the hands of the military and eventually four mid-sized

---

[9] For a powerfully suggestive essay on the ferocity of the Pacific War see John Gregory Dunne, "The Hardest War," *New York Review of Books*, Vol. 48 (December 20, 2001), pp. 50–56. Note that Dunne makes the valuable point (p. 56) that "almost immediately after Hiroshima, the unremitting horror of the Pacific campaign began to slip even what tenuous claim it had on American attention." But the Interim Committee had this "horror" right before them in May–June of 1945.

[10] On racial stereotypes see John W. Dower, *War Without Mercy: Race and Power in the Pacific War* (New York, 1986).

[11] On the work of the Target Committee see Malloy, *Atomic Tragedy*, pp. 116–118.

[12] Malloy, *Atomic Tragedy*, pp. 51, 60–62.

[13] See the discussion in Hewlett and Anderson, Jr., *The New World, 1939–1946*, pp. 358–359.

industrial cities, each containing significant military facilities, were chosen as targets. General Groves, with his customary bluster and intensity, wished to make Kyoto, the ancient capital of Japan, the initial target for the atomic bomb to inflict the maximum psychological shock on the Japanese populace, but Stimson, with Truman's eventual backing, overrode him. Instead the war planners settled on Hiroshima, Kokura, Niigata, and Nagasaki as the primary targets. These cities were saved from conventional bombing because, as Michael Gordin explained, "Groves and his scientific counterparts wanted a 'clean' background against which to judge the effects of the bomb, [and because] an undamaged target was more likely to fit into the 'shock' strategy by showing the significance of this single weapon."[14]

Immediately after the Interim Committee's June 1 meeting Byrnes left the Pentagon and hurried to the White House where he personally briefed Truman on its conclusions. At this meeting the two men reviewed the estimates of American casualties should an invasion of Japan take place and, as David Robertson put it, "the likelihood that the shock of an unannounced atomic attack would force Japan to surrender unconditionally without the necessity of the two invasions [planned for Kyushu and Honshu]."[15] These two politicians saw the matter clearly. Moral complexities or future diplomatic implications failed to complicate their straightforward thinking. The atomic bomb might possibly save American lives if it could be successfully tested and then delivered upon its Japanese targets. This remained, throughout, the essential motivation that guided the decision to use the horrific weapon against Hiroshima and Nagasaki in August of 1945.

Truman received other briefings on the work of the Interim Committee, but Byrnes proved to be his key adviser. When Stimson saw him on June 6 to brief him on the committee's labors Truman admitted "that Byrnes had reported to him already about it and that Byrnes seemed to be highly pleased with what had been done." Stimson attempted to instruct Truman on the potential bargaining power of the new weapon, especially with regard to the Soviet Union. He explained that "no disclosure of the work should be made to anyone until all promises of control were made and established," and then discussed "further *quid pro quos* which should be established in consideration for our taking them [the Soviets] into the partnership." Far from being a recipe for atomic intimidation, Stimson's approach, which in retrospect appears sadly naive, saw the potential

[14] Gordin, *Five Days in August*, pp. 44–45.   [15] Robertson, *Sly and Able*, p. 411.

sharing of the new weapon as a means to foster Soviet cooperation through diplomatic trade-offs. Stimson's increasing obsession with the diplomatic implications of the possible new weapon led to his raising the issue whenever he got near Truman. The president appeared not to share his secretary of war's obsession. He humored Stimson on June 6 by agreeing that he had given some thought to the quid pro quo approach, but then redirected the conversation to "the accomplishment which Harry Hopkins had made in Moscow," relating to Stalin's Far Eastern promises.[16] In fact Truman preferred to keep some distance from the detailed discussions on the use of the atomic bomb. He trusted Byrnes and followed his counsel.

Untold gallons of ink have been spilled to facilitate discussion and debate over the decision to use the bomb, but the actual decision proceeded forward rather smoothly. Reading backwards as citizens of the atomic age, historians have given the decision to use this devastating weapon an importance that it didn't obtain at the time. As the astute Robert James Maddox has noted, among the responsible decision makers "there was no debate over *whether* to use the bomb when it became available; the question was *how*."[17] This crucial point is endorsed by the Stanford historian Barton Bernstein when explaining why "there was no need for an actual 'decision' meeting" to use the bomb. "Such a meeting," Bernstein noted, "would have been required if there had been a serious question about whether or not to use the bomb on Japan. [But] no one at or near the top of the U.S. government raised such a question; no one at the top objected before Hiroshima and Nagasaki to use of the weapon on the enemy."[18] The dissenting scientists simply didn't rate in the eyes of the policy makers who bore responsibility for winning the war.

Whatever the subsequent controversy, Truman had to make no profound and wrenching decision to use the atomic weapon. While certain scientists like Szilard were filled with anguish, there is little evidence for the president's agonizing over the matter. This was a "buck" that came to his desk merely so that he could endorse the consensus of his advisers. The president showed no inclination to question in any way the guiding, if implied, assumption that had prevailed under his predecessor's administration that the bomb was a weapon of war built to be used. His willingness to authorize the dropping of the atomic bomb placed him in a direct

---

[16] Stimson memorandum of conversation with the President, June 6, 1945, Papers of Henry S. Stimson, Yale University. See also entry for June 6, 1945, Stimson Diaries.

[17] Robert James Maddox, *The United States and World War II* (Boulder, CO, 1992), p. 305.

[18] Barton J. Bernstein, "Commentary" in H-Diplo Roundtable on Tsuyoshi Hasegawa's *Racing the Enemy*, p. 15.

continuity with FDR for, as Gerhard Weinberg has argued, "nothing suggests that Roosevelt, had he lived, would have decided differently."[19] Truman's "decision" ultimately was, as General Leslie Groves of the Manhattan Project later suggested, the negative one of not interfering in a course already charted and powerfully driven. Perhaps Groves went too far in suggesting that so powerful were the forces that they carried Truman forward to the use of the bomb "like a little boy on a taboggan" careening downhill.[20] Yet, one must acknowledge that Truman possessed neither the capacity nor the desire to question the logic of the bomb's use.

Whatever the hopes for atomic weapons, the American military in no way built its strategy to defeat Japan on the successful testing and use of them. To achieve this ultimate goal the Americans forcefully pursued a number of strategies – tightening the naval blockade of the Japanese home islands, continuing a massive conventional bombing assault by General Curtis LeMay's B-29s, which rained incendiary napalm bombs on Japanese cities, and preparing for an invasion and subsequent ground war. The Pacific War had been fought with a savage intensity from the outset but in the latter months of 1944 and the early months of 1945 it took on dimensions of brutality that turned its battlefields into what one writer rightly termed "killing grounds of unusual ferocity."[21] From a conventional military perspective the U.S. Navy had inflicted a devastating defeat on the Japanese fleet at the Battle of Leyte Gulf in October–November, 1944. Thereafter, the U.S. forces consolidated their control of the sea and the air as they moved closer and closer to Japan. While such circumstances presaged eventual defeat for Japan, they prompted no weakening of Japanese resolve. Quite the opposite occurred. Leyte saw the introduction by the Japanese of *kamikaze* attacks on American ships and these suicide air strikes proved a grave threat to American forces as the war progressed. They certainly increased significantly the numbers of American casualties and clarified for American forces that Japan would fight to the bitter end.

The fierce and suicidal resistance of the Japanese was hardly restricted to the young pilots of the Divine Wind Special Attack Corps. On land in a

---

[19] Gerhard L. Weinberg, *A World At Arms: A Global History of World War II* (New York, 1994), p. 573.

[20] Leslie R. Groves, *Now It Can Be Told: The Story of the Manhattan Project* (New York, 1962), pp. 264–266. Groves's "boy on a taboggan" reference is quoted from John Newhouse, *War and Peace in the Nuclear Age* (New York, 1989), p. 43.

[21] Eric Bergerud, "No Quarter: The Pacific Battlefield," *Historically Speaking* (June, 2002), p. 9.

series of ghastly and bloody battles the American forces met relentless opposition. The Japanese viewed surrender with contempt and fought accordingly. Also, as the British writer Max Hastings noted in his brilliant study *Retribution: The Battle for Japan, 1944–45*, by this point in the war "the indispensable qualification for high command [in the Japanese military] was a willingness to fight heedless of circumstances, and to avow absolute faith in victory."[22] A bloodbath is hardly too strong a term to describe what took place in 1945 as General MacArthur's troops fought the Japanese in Manila and throughout Luzon. And perhaps wholesale carnage barely suffices to capture the fighting that occurred as Admiral Chester Nimitz's fleets moved ahead to capture key islands in the Bonin and Ryukyu chains, which might be needed as air or staging bases for the invasion of the home islands.

Iwo Jima was a mere speck of land in the vast waters of the Pacific, a tiny island barely five miles long and two and half miles wide, but strategically located approximately seven hundred miles from Tokyo. The Japanese committed 21,000 troops to its defense and they burrowed into caves, an elaborate system of tunnels, and reinforced bunkers to withstand the pounding from aerial bombardment and the shelling from the U.S. fleet. They greeted the Marine divisions that invaded the island with tenacious opposition and fought virtually to the last man during late February and March of 1945. They inflicted enormous casualties on the Americans – more than 6,000 dead and 20,000 wounded. The Marines raised the stars and stripes on Mount Surabachi quite early in the battle, but the Iwo Jima operation took longer than expected and the price proved extremely high. Worse was to come.

Okinawa was a much bigger island than Iwo Jima and was located a mere 350 miles from Japan. U.S. planners deemed it a crucial springboard for the planned invasion of Kyushu. It was defended by a Japanese force of over 100,000 troops of whom about a quarter were local Okinawa militia. The troops also drew on the support of hundreds of *kamikazes* who flew from bases on the home islands. The Japanese referred to the battle as "rain of steel" and that certainly describes what descended upon them prior to the invasion of U.S. land forces. The U.S. forces under the command of Lieut. Gen. Simon Bolivar Buckner, Jr., came ashore on April 1, 1945, and vicious fighting ensued for the next 82 days until American victory was achieved. By the time the fighting stopped in late June the Japanese had suffered hideous casualties. Only 7,000 Japanese soldiers

---

[22] Max Hastings, *Retribution: The Battle for Japan, 1944–45* (New York, 2008), p. 58.

surrendered and survived and a good number of these were from the Okinawan militia. Additionally, somewhere between 50,000 to 150,000 noncombatant Okinawans died in the horrendous clash, including some who committed mass suicide to avoid capture by the Americans whom they believed would commit horrible atrocities against them. The Americans suffered fewer losses but they were still horrendous, reaching over 70,000 casualties of whom 12,000 were killed or missing. Among those killed were General Buckner and the famous war correspondent Ernie Pyle. The *kamikaze* attacks proved effective and sank 36 American ships including 12 destroyers. The U.S. losses included almost 5,000 sailors killed and a similar number wounded. When the awful tabulating of losses was completed Okinawa stood as the bloodiest battle that U.S. forces fought in the Pacific War and as the second bloodiest of World War II after the Battle of the Bulge.[23]

At Iwo Jima and Okinawa the Japanese forced the Americans to pay an enormous price for their military success and they gave no indication of altering their resolution to die rather than to surrender and accept defeat. Whatever their own appalling losses they appeared determined to fight unrelentingly in defense of their homeland. Even the enhanced and brutally destructive bombing campaign of the Twenty-First Bomber Command under Maj. Gen. Curtis LeMay did not dent their resolve. Operating out of the Mariana Islands from February–March 1945, LeMay fully adopted the strategies of area bombing and targeting of cities. Following experimental raids against Kobe and Tokyo in February, the Americans launched a massive firebombing raid against Tokyo on March 9. Over 100,000 people were killed and sixteen square miles of the city destroyed in the fierce blaze started by the incendiary bombs. In May and June LeMay's planes bombed not only Japan's largest cities such as Tokyo, Nagoya, Osaka, and Yokohama, but many medium-sized cities with populations over 100,000. The high civilian casualties and the huge physical destruction, however, failed to persuade the military leaders of Japan to sue for peace. American military planners concluded that a Japanese surrender would come only after the invasion of the home islands. The human toll of such an invasion began to appear ever more costly.

In mid-June 1945, as the fighting on Okinawa entered its final phase, Truman received the unanimous recommendation of the Joint Chiefs of

---

[23] For casualty figures see Michael Kort, "Casualty Projections for the Invasion of Japan, Phantom Estimates, and the Math of Barton Bernstein," *Passport: The Newsletter of the Society for Historians of American Foreign Relations*, Vol. 34 (December, 2003) pp. 7, 9.

Staff for the invasion. Operation Olympic, a fourteen-division operation, provided for attacks on the southern island of Kyushu beginning November 1. Operation Coronet, which would involve twenty-four divisions, set out plans for a later major assault on the Tokyo plain of the main island of Honshu tentatively scheduled for March 1, 1946. Casualties from these military exercises were expected to be high. Although Truman's later suggestion that he received advice that the United States might suffer a million casualties has been contested by some historians, "there is no question that Truman thought casualties would be heavy," as Robert James Maddox noted.[24] And the indefatigable research of D. M. Giangreco clarifies that former president Herbert Hoover's warning to Truman in late May that the invasion could cost from half a million to a million lives was taken very seriously by the president.[25] Indeed he feared "an Okinawa from one end of Japan to the other."[26]

Hoover's huge casualty projections weighed heavily on Truman and colored his preparation for a meeting with his senior military and civilian advisers on June 18 where he finalized the military planning for the Pacific War. A few days before this meeting Admiral Leahy alerted the joint chiefs of staff of the president's desire for "an estimate of the time required and an estimate of the losses in killed and wounded that will result from an invasion of Japan." Leahy explained that the commander in chief wished to pursue a campaign "with the purpose of economizing to the maximum extent possible in the loss of American lives."[27] Truman's anxiety over the prospect of high American casualties caused some anxiety in turn among American military planners, who worried about the president's commitment to the invasion strategy they had developed.[28]

There was good reason for Truman's concern, and the American military commanders increasingly began to appreciate this. Through the ULTRA code-breaking efforts they had access to Japanese military planning and during May and June they observed a steady buildup of Japanese forces on Kyushu. While the Japanese high command did not enjoy a similar advantage of being able to track American military planning,

---

[24] Maddox, *The United States and World War II*, p. 306. I rely on Maddox for some of the factual details in the preceding sentences.

[25] Giangreco, *Hell to Pay*, pp. 79–81.

[26] Minutes of meeting, June 18, 1945, *FRUS: Potsdam, 1945*, (Washington, D.C., 1960), I, p. 909.

[27] Leahy memorandum to Joint Chiefs of Staff, June 14, 1945, quoted in Douglas J. MacEachin, *The Final Months of the War with Japan: Signals Intelligence, U.S. Invasion Planning and the A-Bomb Decision* (Langley, VA, 1998), p. 11.

[28] See MacEachin, *The Final Months of the War with Japan*, pp. 12–13.

they knew an invasion was coming and they guessed correctly that the beaches of Kyushu would be the likely landing areas. They determined, as Edward Drea has appositely remarked, "to convert these beachheads into graveyards for American troops." As of June the ULTRA intercepts were telling two related stories. "One was a straightforward rendition of Tokyo's hurried efforts to transform Kyushu into a mighty bastion," as Drea explained. "The other," he astutely noted, "was even more frightening. Nowhere in the enemy's mindset could ULTRA detect pessimism or defeatism. Instead Japan's military leaders were determined to go down fighting and take as many Americans with them as possible."[29]

The Japanese planned to implement their *Ketsu-Go* (Decisive Operation) strategy, which would employ the combined strength of the Japanese army, navy, and air forces to meet the anticipated attacks on the sacred soil of their homeland. The Japanese had been surprised by "the seemingly relentless character of the American advance," but as Giangreco explains at length, this didn't deter them. They calculated that they could inflict such punishment on American forces that they would lose heart for the struggle and agree to peace terms. Through 1945 the Japanese instituted increases in conscription and raised new divisions. Additionally, they moved experienced troops back home from Manchuria, China, and Korea. The Japanese had waged the war they began with notable fierceness from the outset. But as the invasion of their homeland approached, attrition warfare or "bloodletting operations" were adopted as essential tactics to greet any invading force.[30] Capturing the home islands rightly appeared a daunting task. Stanley Weintraub does not exaggerate when he notes that "Okinawa was not a worst-case scenario" but rather a prelude to "the far more extensive killing ground of Japan."[31]

Prior to the June 18 meeting General Marshall, in response to Truman's queries, had requested Gen. Douglas MacArthur to provide an updated estimate of the American casualties for Operation Olympic. MacArthur's initial response of 105,500 battle casualties for the first ninety days plus 12,600 more nonbattle losses shocked Marshall who feared its impact on Truman's resolve.[32] At the June 18 meeting to obtain approval for

---

[29] See Edward Drea's brilliant essay "Intelligence Forecasting for the Invasion of Japan: Previews of Hell," in his *In the Service of the Emperor: Essays on the Imperial Japanese Army* (Lincoln, NE, 1998), pp. 156–157.

[30] Giangreco, *Hell to Pay*, pp. 32, 97 ff., 12.

[31] Stanley Weintraub, "Three Colonels: A Foreword," in Ginagreco, *Hell to Pay*, p. xi.

[32] I rely on Drea for these numbers and the following analysis. See his *In the Service of the Emperor*, p. 157.

Olympic he understated the likely casualty figures, and vaguely suggested that "there is reason to believe that the first 30 days in Kyushu should not exceed the price we have paid for Luzon." In making his case for the Olympic operation, however, Marshall drew not on MacArthur's specific casualty estimates but on the Pacific commander's overall analysis that the Olympic operation "presents less hazards of excessive loss than any other that has been suggested and that its decisive effect will eventually save lives by eliminating wasteful operations of nondecisive character." The Kyushu invasion represented "the most economical one in effort and lives that is possible." In case the president missed the point that he was presenting what he judged the best among a number of bloody options to force Japan's surrender, Marshall noted "the grim fact that there was not an easy, bloodless way to victory in war and it is the thankless task of the leaders to maintain their firm outward front which holds the resolution of their subordinates."[33]

Flinty old Admiral Leahy provided a more realistic numerical assessment of likely losses suggesting that Kyushu would mirror Okinawa where the casualty rate reached approximately 35 percent of troops employed. After clarifying that over three quarters of a million soldiers would be committed to Kyushu he left Truman to do his own calculation. Yet, Leahy did not oppose Operation Olympic, and after some brief questioning Truman accepted the unanimous Joint Chiefs recommendation, "after weighing all the possibilities of the situation and considering all possible alternative plans, ... that the Kyushu operation is the best solution under the circumstances."[34] While Operation Olympic got the immediate go-ahead, he reserved Operation Coronet for a later final decision.

In approving the invasion plans the American leaders had deemed the naval blockade and continued bombing as insufficient to bring about Japanese capitulation at the lowest cost and within an acceptable time frame. American troops would have to wade ashore just as they had done at Luzon, Iwo Jima, and Okinawa. Given that prospect, Marshall affirmed the value of gaining Russian participation in the conflict so that the Red Army could "deal with the Japs in Manchuria (and Korea if necessary)," and Truman reassured the group that one of his objectives at the upcoming Potsdam meeting "would be to get from Russia all the assistance in the war

---

[33] Minutes of meeting, June 18, 1945, *FRUS: Potsdam, 1945,* I, p. 905.
[34] Minutes of meeting, June 18, 1945, *FRUS: Potsdam, 1945,* I, p. 908.

that was possible."[35] Interestingly the prospect of obtaining the atomic bombs never entered into the central discussions of Truman and his military planners at this meeting. These weapons still could not be relied upon for purposes of military planning and strategy.

Other issues surfaced at the June 18 meeting. Admiral Leahy tried to question the unconditional surrender terms being held out before the Japanese, but Truman evaded the issue by deeming it a topic for Congress to address. He implied, however, that American public opinion would not tolerate any change in such conditions.[36] Truman seemed more open to a suggestion from Assistant Secretary of War John J. McCloy that Japan should be warned of the impending use of a "terrifyingly destructive weapon" and also given some indication that they might be permitted to retain the emperor on the basis of a constitutional monarchy. According to McCloy's later account Truman agreeably encouraged him to take his suggestions up with Byrnes. The proposal for a warning gained support, but his latter idea regarding the emperor met a less than enthusiastic reception with the South Carolinian. Byrnes thought the proposal might be viewed by the Japanese as weakness on the American part, which might only encourage their continued resistance. He advised McCloy that he "would oppose any 'deal' as a concomitant of a demand for surrender."[37] And that was the end of it, because as June came to an end Jimmy Byrnes ruled the deck of the Truman administration's foreign policy ship. He had helped chart the course for Truman on the use of the atomic bomb, but his portfolio now expanded rapidly as he assumed the duties of secretary of state.

Truman relished having Byrnes in charge of foreign policy matters. He held no lengthy session briefing for his new secretary on his hopes and expectations in the foreign policy realm. Rather he expected Byrnes to brief himself on the pressing issues and then to guide the administration's foreign policy. The new secretary of state took office at a time when numerous issues demanded attention and with his departure for a major international conference less than a week away. A less capable person might have faltered, but Byrnes pushed forward with preparations for

---

[35] Minutes of meeting, June 18, 1945, *FRUS: Potsdam, 1945*, I, pp. 905, 909.

[36] Minutes of meeting, June 18, 1945, *FRUS: Potsdam, 1945*, I, p. 909.

[37] For McCloy's recollections of the June 18 meeting and his subsequent meeting with Byrnes see "McCloy on the A-Bomb" included as an appendix in James Reston, *Deadline: A Memoir* (New York, 1992), pp. 495–500. Also see John J. McCloy, *The Challenge to American Foreign Policy* (Cambridge, 1953), pp. 41–43; and McCloy's comments to Forrestal in Walter Millis, ed., *The Forrestal Diaries* (New York, 1951), pp. 70–71.

the Potsdam meeting. His independence, pragmatism, and tactical skill stood him in good stead. He came to his new office without any grand strategic vision. Tactics rather than strategy were his forte, but he brought with him over three decades of experience as a negotiator. He prepared to put that talent to special use at Potsdam.

CHAPTER 4

The Potsdam Conference, the Trinity Test, and Atomic Diplomacy

The Potsdam Conference holds a rather hazy place in American memory. This last of the three wartime conferences of the leaders of the Soviet Union, Great Britain, and the United States took place in the latter half of July 1945 in the Berlin suburb from whence it drew its name. Details of the conference agreements are shrouded in a fog of ignorance and even capable historians rarely present Potsdam as an especially memorable affair. The greatest drama associated with it rests in it having supposedly served as the venue for atomic diplomacy.[1] Yet, a close examination of the conference deliberations reveals an American effort, spearheaded by the new Secretary of State James F. Byrnes, but bearing Truman's endorsement, to negotiate something approaching "a spheres of influence peace." As Marc Trachtenberg astutely emphasized, Potsdam constituted an important step toward the division of Europe "as the basis of the postwar international order."[2] Such a division was not the painful consequence of the failure of negotiations but the very object and culmination of these negotiations. Byrnes led the way at Potsdam in tough bargaining with the Soviets designed to settle some of the major issues that the victorious powers confronted, in particular the future of Germany. Understanding the Byrnes-Truman approach at Potsdam is essential for grasping the real

---

[1] This is the view offered most notably and dramatically by Gar Alperovitz in *Atomic Diplomacy: Hiroshima and Potsdam* (rev. ed.). The earliest version of this book was subjected to a devastating critique by Robert James Maddox who incisively noted the misleading use of sources by its author. See Maddox, *The New Left and the Origins of the Cold War* (Princeton, NJ, 1973), pp. 63–78.

[2] See the chapter, "A Spheres of Influence Peace?" in Marc Trachtenberg, *A Constructed Peace: The Making of the European Settlement, 1945–1963* (Princeton, NJ, 1999), p. 14.

nature of American diplomacy at this crucial time. It also allows for a clear evaluation of the extent to which news of the successful test of the first atomic weapon influenced American planning to defeat Japan and its policy toward the Soviet Union.

After his lightning and unanimous approval by the Senate, Byrnes enjoyed a rather festive swearing-in ceremony on July 3 in the Rose Garden of the White House. Surrounded by his friends, he swore his oath using his wife's bible, and quickly got to work. He genuinely desired to maintain amicable relations with the Soviet Union. He possessed no sympathy for the more hard-line attitude, which certain state department officials aimed toward the Soviet Union. He proved as open as Truman to the advice of Ambassador Joseph Davies. In late May in response to a rising strain of anti-Soviet commentary in the press, Byrnes had encouraged a fretting Davies to explain to "our Russian friends" that "those in responsible positions are determined to let nothing interfere with the friendly relations existing between our two countries."[3] Davies continued occasional meetings with Byrnes through late June and early July, and clearly a solid connection existed between them. Byrnes requested that Davies join the delegation for Potsdam and the inveterate Soviet sympathizer would sit beside the president, the secretary of state, and Admiral Leahy at the conference table.

While Davies secured an invitation to the Big Three gathering, other senior administration officials still scurried to obtain presidential approval to join the American team in Germany. Notably, Secretary Stimson angled for the opportunity to exercise influence at the conference, but Truman displayed little enthusiasm for his presence. Poor Stimson, the distinguished elder statesman of the cabinet no less, tepidly raised the matter with Truman on July 2 by inquiring if the president feared whether he "could not physically stand the trip."[4] He had spent their meeting yet again instructing Truman on the importance of the atomic bomb to his meeting with Stalin and Churchill and implying the value of his presence to offer counsel on this matter, but Truman tellingly deflected his inquiry and merely promised to consider his request. Nonetheless, Stimson continued to press his views on Truman. In a further meeting with Truman in the Oval Office on July 3 after Byrnes's swearing-in ceremony and acting with the endorsement of the Interim Committee, he advised Truman how to

---

[3] Byrnes quoted in Elizabeth Kimball MacLean, *Joseph E. Davies: Envoy to the Soviets* (Westport, CT, 1992), p. 152.
[4] Stimson Diaries, July 2, 1945.

inform Stalin regarding the atomic bomb.[5] At this meeting Truman relented and invited Stimson to attend the Potsdam meeting, but the secretary of war would not be a full participant in the main negotiating sessions. He merely would be available for consultation.

While Stimson pushed to get to Potsdam, Truman fretted that he had to go. His preference for domestic issues and reticence to engage in international diplomacy became more obvious as the departure date for the summit approached. Few are the American chief executives who privately whined so much about attending an international meeting. "I am getting ready to go see Stalin and Churchill," he wrote to his mother and his sister Mary on July 3. "I have to take my tuxedo, tails, Negro preacher coat, high hat, low hat and hard hat as well as sundry other things. I have a briefcase filled up with information on past conferences and suggestions on what I'm to do and say. Wish I didn't have to go, but I do and it can't be stopped now."[6] On the day of his departure for Europe he confided to his diary: "Talked to Bess last night and the night before. She wasn't happy about my going to see Mr. Russia and Mr. Great Britain – neither am I." He summarized his feelings by exclaiming on paper: "How I hate this trip!"[7]

However reluctantly, Truman geared up to undertake this major international mission and his first trip across the Atlantic since his time in uniform during World War I. The general American approach centered on obtaining agreements and settling the "remaining wartime problems so that U.S. military and economic responsibilities in Europe could be terminated."[8] The Americans, it must be stressed, did not set off with an anti-Soviet disposition. Truman, perhaps with some retrospective exaggeration, recalled that he "went to Potsdam with the kindliest feelings in the world toward Russia."[9] State Department Undersecretary Joseph Grew complained that Churchill's list of proposed topics for the conference "is so drawn as to give the appearance largely of a bill of complaints against the Soviet Government," which he archly noted, "seems hardly the proper approach to the forthcoming meeting."[10] Regardless of their sincere desire for agreements, however, the Truman-Byrnes team went to Potsdam with a different approach to negotiations than the one pursued by Franklin

---

[5] Stimson Diaries, July 3, 1945.   [6] Truman, *Year of Decisions*, p. 367.

[7] Diary entry, July 7, 1945, in Ferrell, ed., *Off the Record*, p. 49.

[8] This is the argument of Randall B. Woods and Howard Jones in their *Dawning of the Cold War: The United States' Quest for Order* (Athens, GA, 1991), p. 58.

[9] Interview with Truman, January 22, 1954, Truman Papers, Post-Presidential Files, Box 643.

[10] Grew to Truman, June 14, 1945, *FRUS: Potsdam, 1945*, I, p. 164.

Roosevelt. Neither Truman nor Byrnes focused either on winning Stalin's trust or coaxing him into concessions. Instead the new American leaders approached their discussions with the Soviets and the British as politicians and practical men eager to reach the best deal they could for their own country. "I'm not working for any interest but the Republic of the United States," Truman confirmed in his diary on the very day the USS *Augusta* set out to carry him and his party across the Atlantic.[11] But the president and his secretary of state essentially saw the representatives of the nations with whom they must deal as mirror images of themselves – practical men with whom a deal could be struck, who would be working for the interests of their respective countries.

Truman and Byrnes considered it especially important that the Potsdam settlement be politically palatable in the United States. On July 6, his final day in Washington before the trip, the president received a memorandum signed by his personal advisers and presidential aides, John Snyder, Sam Rosenman, and George Allen, outlining the "consensus" reached at a meeting they held with Truman on July 4, at which they discussed the important issues for and desired outcomes of the conference. Notably they listed "the entry of Russia into the Japanese War," as the first objective for the president with the "economic stabilization of Europe" listed second. They went on to express to Truman their view that "as a well known Missouri horse trader, the American people expect you to bring something home to them."[12] As he left the United States he referred approvingly to Byrnes as his "able and conniving Secretary of State," adding that he had "a keen mind" and was an "honest man."

By the time Truman's party arrived in Europe they had settled on four major issues upon which they would seek agreement above and beyond the U.S. interest in obtaining Soviet military support against the Japanese. The first involved developing "procedure and machinery for peace negotiations and territorial settlements." Truman and Byrnes had no expectation that Potsdam would serve as the location for fashioning peace treaties with the defeated foes. Rather, it would be the place where agreement could be reached on the process for preparing such treaties. Here lay the basis for the American proposal to establish a council of foreign ministers. Not surprisingly, German matters occupied a crucial place on the American list. The United States would seek to settle on principles to govern the occupation and also would seek a new approach on reparations following

---

[11] Ferrell, ed., *Off the Record*, p. 49.
[12] Snyder, Rosenman, and Allen to Truman, July 6, 1945, *FRUS: Potsdam, 1945*, I, p. 228.

on the failure of the Reparations Commission in Moscow to finalize this matter. Lastly, the Americans wanted agreement on "plans for carrying out the Yalta Declaration on Liberated Europe, with the hope," as Byrnes remembered, "of ending the constant friction which had prevailed over Russian policy in eastern Europe since the Crimea Conference."[13] They had other objectives such as Truman's pet proposal to guarantee free navigation of Europe's inland waterways, but these major issues lay at the core of the American diplomatic purpose at Potsdam. Byrnes eventually would seek to relate them in developing a compromise agreement. Notably, these objectives had not been fashioned in light of the prospect of obtaining an atomic weapon.

On July 14, the USS *Augusta* and its accompanying cruiser, the USS *Philadelphia*, reached British waters off Portsmouth, and the next day the *Augusta* docked in Antwerp where Gen. Dwight Eisenhower met the president and his party. From Belgium the American team flew to Berlin, the seat of the thousand-year Reich, which now lay in ruins. The president and his party then drove to the Babelsberg district of Potsdam where the Soviets had assigned Truman to a yellow stucco villa by a small lake that became the "Little White House." Here he settled in and readied himself for the meetings ahead at the conference to which Churchill, with unwitting insight, had given the code name of "Terminal." The symbolic overtones and implications of this code name should not disguise the fact that Truman thought this would be but the first of a series of meetings to secure the peace.

Portrayals of the Potsdam Conference usually focus on the interactions of the principals Truman, Stalin, and Churchill, whose place as prime minister was taken by Clement Attlee midway through the meeting. Their conversations and the formal meetings around the conference table at the Cecilienhof Palace, once the estate of the former Crown Prince Wilhelm, hold their own importance, but they were not central to the ultimate outcome of the meeting. The essential discussions took place one level down and James F. Byrnes played the crucial role in designing the final settlement. He, not Truman, proved to be the principal American negotiator, a role he undertook with the president's approval. Of course Churchill and Stalin were both eager to meet Franklin Roosevelt's successor and preliminary sessions were held before the formal beginning of the conference. Truman also took the chance to tour the remnants of Berlin. Observing the damage the president observed accurately: "Hitler's folly."[14]

[13] Byrnes, *Speaking Frankly*, pp. 67–68.
[14] Truman diary entry, July 16, 1945, in Ferrell, ed., *Off the Record*, p. 51.

Stalin had arrived in Potsdam on July 16 and came to the Little White House right before noon on July 17. After initial pleasantries the American and Soviet leaders "got down to business" according to Truman's account. Truman explained that he was "no diplomat" but wanted to answer "yes or no" on hearing the arguments. He straightforwardly assured Stalin of his friendship. So assured, Stalin, with his usual negotiating skill, set forth a number of items for the conference agenda that might be considered a reach even for a man of his voracious appetite for power and control. Truman referred to them as "dynamite," presumably for their likely explosive impact on Churchill. The Soviet leader mentioned removing Franco's fascist government in Spain, the appropriate disposition of Italian colonies in North Africa, and obtaining a share of the German fleet. In a bid to gain American goodwill and perhaps also to clarify the American need for Soviet support against Japan, the generalissimo maligned Churchill and the British effort in the Pacific War and suggested that now the Russians and the Americans could form an alliance to defeat Japan while Great Britain had little to offer.[15] Truman welcomed the assurances of Soviet participation in the Pacific War. He observed in his diary that evening regarding the Soviet commitment to declare war against Japan in mid-August that it would mean "fini Japs (sic) when that comes about."[16] The exact meaning of this late-night diary entry has been much debated and probably overly so. The remark most likely points to nothing more than Truman's excitement that Soviet entry would hurry along the defeat of Japan. The suggestion that this comment illustrates a belief that Soviet entry would be sufficient, of itself, to bring about Japan's defeat seems far-fetched. As J. Samuel Walker has noted, the military guidance that Truman received held that "an invasion or 'imminent' invasion, combined with Soviet participation in the war," would be required to bring about Japan's defeat.[17] His diary entry should be interpreted in light of this military advice.

Truman appreciated his meeting with Stalin. "I can deal with Stalin," he reassured himself, and then offered the partially flawed assessment that "he is honest – but smart as hell."[18] The Missouri trader seemed to believe that

---

[15] This summary of the first Truman-Stalin meeting relies upon Bohlen's cryptic notes printed in Charles L. Mee, *Meeting at Potsdam* (New York, 1975), pp. 90–94; and Truman's diary entry, July 17, 1945, in Ferrell, ed., *Off the Record*, p. 53.

[16] Diary entry, July 17, 1945, in Ferrell, ed., *Off the Record*, p. 53.

[17] J. Samuel Walker, "Recent Literature on Truman's Atomic Bomb Decision: A Search for Middle Ground," *Diplomatic History*, 29 (April, 2005), p. 320.

[18] Diary entry, July 17, 1945, in Ferrell, ed., *Off the Record*, p. 53.

Stalin's "honesty" bore a certain resemblance to that of a tough political boss in the United States like Tom Pendergast, an analogy both astoundingly naïve and ample grounds for poor Boss Tom, whatever his many flaws, to pursue legal action for defamation of character were he still alive.[19] Truman's regard and even affection for Stalin was genuine and surfaced on subsequent occasions, most famously during his 1948 campaign when he publicly admitted: "I like old Joe," and went on to brand him "a prisoner of the Politburo."[20] He hardly approached Stalin warily as a harsh dictator let alone as one of the world's greatest moral monsters. Just like FDR he wanted to secure Soviet-American friendship in the postwar years and to firm up Soviet participation in the war against Japan. On July 18 Truman wrote to his wife that "I've gotten what I came for – Stalin goes to war August 15 with no strings on it.... I'll say that we'll end the war a year sooner now, and think of the kids who won't be killed! That is the important thing."[21] Indeed, it truly was *the* most important thing for Truman.

The deep and constant concern to assure the defeat of Japan caused Truman and Byrnes to track events occurring thousands of miles away in the deserts of New Mexico. Early in the morning of July 16 at "Trinity," the code name for the Manhattan Project test site in Alamogordo, a group of officials and scientists led by General Groves and Robert Oppenheimer readied themselves for the initial test of the weapon upon which the scientists had expended such energy. The historian Mark Fiege has suggested that the "name of the test site reflected the atomic scientists' cosmic and eschatological vision." He notes that some "probably called to mind the Father, Son, and Holy Ghost of Christian belief," but for Oppenheimer, "reader of Sanskrit and the *Bhagavad Gita*, it may have evoked the Hindu trinity of Brahma, Vishnu, and Shiva." He further observed that "for Hindus as for physicists, matter and energy are never ultimately destroyed; they are only transformed."[22]

The first full-scale test was made of the implosion type fission atomic bomb. It was not dropped from a plane but was exploded on a platform atop a 100-foot-high steel tower. Oppenheimer himself had climbed the

[19] On Truman's view of Stalin as a tough political boss see Deborah Welch Larson, *Origins of Containment: A Psychological Explanation* (Princeton, NJ, 1985), pp. 177–178.

[20] For the quote and further discussion of the 1948 episode see Clark Clifford with Richard Holbrooke, *Counsel to the President: A Memoir* (New York, 1991), pp. 200–201.

[21] Truman letter, July 18, 1945, in Robert H. Ferrell, ed., *Dear Bess: The Letters from Harry to Bess Truman, 1910–1959* (New York, 1959), p. 519.

[22] Mark Fiege, "The Atomic Scientists, the Sense of Wonder, and the Bomb," *Environmental History*, Vol. 12, No. 3 (July, 2007), p. 600.

PHOTO 3. The initial atomic device waits at the base of the tower to be raised to its firing position. Trinity Test, Alamogordo, New Mexico, July 16, 1945. (Courtesy Harry S. Truman Presidential Library.)

tower to give the bomb his final inspection and then moved to his protected observation shelter over five miles away. General Groves was on hand to calm his tense Los Alamos director. One of Groves' military aides, Brig. Thomas F. Farrell, remembered the tension inside the shelter among the scientists who "felt that their figuring must be right and that the bomb had to go off but there was in everyone's mind a strong measure of doubt." Farrell thought that even some of the atheists present were praying that "the shot" would be successful. Oppenheimer grew tense as the seconds ticked off and held on to a post to steady himself. Then at precisely 5:30 A.M. the world's first atomic bomb was detonated. The observers saw the dramatic flash of light and the huge fireball and felt the shockwaves from the explosion almost a minute after the light had flashed. The huge ball of fire formed into a mushroom cloud, which, as General Groves later reported, "surged and billowed upwards with tremendous power" until it reached the stratosphere.

Robert Oppenheimer later claimed that a line from the *Bahgavad Gita* passed through his mind: "Now I am become Death, the shatterer of

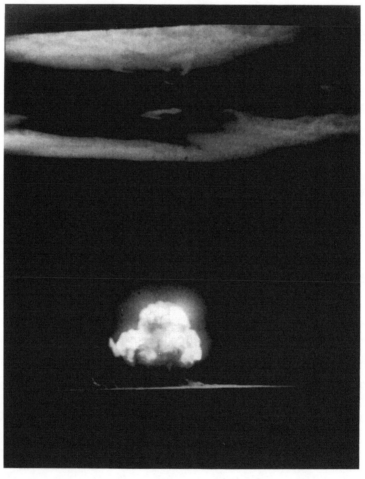

PHOTO 4. The first atomic bomb test, near Alamogordo, New Mexico, July 16, 1945. (Courtesy Harry S. Truman Presidential Library.)

PHOTO 5. The fireball of the Trinity explosion, .053 seconds after detonation as it shook the New Mexico desert, July 16, 1945. (Courtesy Harry S. Truman Presidential Library.)

worlds." Perhaps so, and this recollection allowed him to appear as "having suffered a sense of deep sin at the moment" of the Trinity test.[23] If he so suffered, however, he never made it clear to his brother Frank who stood near him at Alamogordo, and who recalled that they both simply noted that it had worked. General Farrell observed that Oppenheimer's face "relaxed into an expression of tremendous relief" when the bomb exploded. The tension in the room relaxed and the scientists congratulated each other. The chemist George Kistiakowsky even "threw his arms around Oppenheimer and embraced him with shouts of glee." Oppenheimer had been the leader and driving force for the scientists working in that isolated area and he must surely have taken some pride in the success of their accomplishment. Whatever his inner thoughts he never raised questions about using these

[23] I borrow this from Lynn Eden in her thoughtful review of Charles Thorpe's *Oppenheimer: The Tragic Intellect* (2006), in *American Historical Review*, Vol. 113, No. 2 (April, 2008), p. 531.

weapons against Japan. Rather, he worked diligently to assess the power of the weapon he had helped create in preparation for its use in war.[24]

The observers judged the bomb a success beyond their expectations. It released an explosive force of somewhere approaching 20,000 tons of TNT. The test tower simply evaporated. The light and sound of the explosion registered over a hundred miles away. On closer inspection they noted severe destruction well over a half mile from the bomb's crater. Groves quickly conveyed word of the test to Stimson's aide George Harrison who relayed on the news to the secretary of war in cryptic fashion: "Operated on this morning. Diagnosis not yet complete but results seem satisfactory and already exceed expectations."[25] Stimson, filled with excitement, gave Truman a preliminary report in the evening after the president's return from his tour of Berlin. The reality of the bomb in no way altered Truman's decision to use it. It simply, as he reportedly said, took a "great load" off his mind.[26]

Stimson briefed Byrnes at some length on the atomic test the next morning and tried to persuade him that the United States now should alter its plan to utilize the new weapon. Aware of the existence of Japanese peace "feelers" and their efforts to use the Russians as intermediaries, Stimson argued that the combination of a strong warning about the bomb and a firm assurance that the Japanese could retain their emperor might suffice to bring about a Japanese capitulation.[27] Through their MAGIC decryption operation the United States had cracked the Japanese code for diplomatic correspondence, just as the ULTRA operation gave the United States access to Japanese military communications. Thus, American officials now followed the exchanges between Japanese Foreign Minister Shigenori Togo and Japanese Ambassador in Moscow Naotake Sato regarding using the Russians to explore peace terms. On July 15 Ambassador Sato argued: "In the long run, since Japan sincerely desires the termination of the war, I believe that she has indeed no choice but to accept unconditional surrender or terms

---

[24] For Groves's and Farrell's observations quoted in this paragraph see Grove to Secretary of War, July 18, 1945, Papers of Lansing Lamont, in Dennis Merrill, *Documentary History of the Truman Presidency*, Vol. 1, *The Decision to Drop the Atomic Bomb on Japan* (Bethesda, MD, 1995) pp. 122–136.

[25] Harrison to Stimson (War Dept. 32887), July 16, 1945, quoted in Mee, *Meeting at Potsdam*, p. 86.

[26] Diary, July 16, 1945, Davies Papers, Box 18.

[27] See transcripts of these messages for July 2, July 5, July 11, July 12, July 15, 1945, in Byrnes Papers, Folder 571.

closely approximate thereto," (although even he wished to preserve the Japanese "national structure," which meant not simply the emperor as some sort of figurehead but some continuation of the emperor system). Regrettably, the Japanese government rejected his conciliatory advice. On July 21, Foreign Minister Togo responded to the ambassador in Moscow that "with regard to unconditional surrender ... we are unable to consent to it under any circumstances whatsoever. Even if the war drags on and it becomes clear that it will take much more bloodshed, the whole country as one man will pit itself against the enemy in accordance with the Imperial Will so long as the enemy demands unconditional surrender."[28] The Japanese sought not a surrender but rather a negotiated peace to preserve the imperial system, whatever the cost to their own people.

Strongly influenced by former Secretary of State Cordell Hull, Byrnes bluntly rejected both ideas.[29] Byrnes, the experienced politician, saw twin dangers for himself and for the president he served in such proposals. On the one hand retreating from the unconditional surrender terms might be exploited by the Japanese as a sign of American war weariness and cause a political firestorm among a public that held no love for Japan or its ruler. On the other hand not taking advantage of measures that might bring the war to a speedy end and prevent further American casualties would leave him and Truman vulnerable to harsh later criticism. From Byrnes's perspective using the atomic bomb addressed both dangers. It allowed the United States to maintain the surrender terms it had set forth and yet gave some promise of a quicker end to the struggle. Byrnes easily ignored the hand-wringing of Stimson and others, and with Truman's general endorsement proceeded forward with his diplomatic machinations.

Flushed with the news from Alamogordo, Byrnes and Truman now speculated that the imminent atomic attacks on Japan might bring about a surrender prior to the planned Soviet entry into the Pacific War. After talking over matters with Byrnes and others, the president expressed the belief in his diary that "Japs will fold up before Russia comes in. I am sure they will when Manhattan appears over their homeland."[30] Truman took

---

[28] MAGIC intercepts Nos. 1210 and 1212, which contain the translations of the Sato message of July 15 and the Togo message of July 21, can be found in Kort, ed., *The Columbia Guide to Hiroshima and the Bomb*, pp. 283–285.

[29] See the Hull-Byrnes exchange, July 16–17, 1945, in *FRUS: Potsdam, 1945*, II, pp. 1267–1268. For a discussion of the broader debate in the Truman administration over unconditional surrender see Richard B. Frank, *Downfall: The End of the Imperial Japanese Empire* (New York, 1999), pp. 214–220.

[30] Diary entry, July 18, 1945, in Ferrell, ed., *Off the Record*, p. 54.

this as positive news, but he made no moves to depreciate or curtail Soviet participation in the war. His attitude seems to have been that the Allies should apply all possible force to compel Japan's surrender. He wrote his wife on July 20 that he wanted "the Jap war won and I want 'em [Great Britain and the Soviet Union] both in it."[31] In some contrast Byrnes now saw the possession of the atomic bomb as having diplomatic implications. As further confirmation of the bomb's explosive force arrived over the coming days he altered his *attitude* toward Soviet entry into the war against Japan.[32] Byrnes's associate Walter Brown recorded in his diary on July 19 that "JFB determined to out maneuver Stalin on China. Hopes Soong will stand firm and then the Russians will not go in war. Then he feels Japan will surrender before Russia goes to war and this will save China." His biographer portrayed him as an "atomic *diplomat*," when pursuing his diplomatic strategy concerning the Far East.[33] Yet, this effort bears little resemblance to the elaborate and fanciful scheme posited by Gar Alperovitz and company. It reveals only Byrnes's tactical approach and recognition that he would not need to force the Chinese into excessive concessions to Stalin's heavy demands to secure Soviet entry into the war against Japan. He merely reacted quickly to new developments and undertook new approaches to further American ends. Ultimately, however, his supposed attempt at "atomic diplomacy" was not to mean much.

While Truman and Byrnes came to terms with the meaning and implications of having atomic weapons in the American arsenal, the Potsdam Conference formally began on the evening of July 17 the first of its thirteen plenary sessions. Much of the real work of the conference took place away from the formal sessions in lengthy negotiations between Foreign Ministers Eden, Molotov, and Byrnes. The foreign ministers hashed out issues and tried to settle on proposals that could be presented to their principals in the late afternoon meetings in the conference room. The constant referral of matters to the foreign ministers even prompted Stalin to joke to his opposites that "we will have nothing to do."[34] The use of the foreign ministers, however, could not prevent the surfacing at the conference table of the major issues that divided the three powers. Most of these related to Germany and to Poland and more broadly to the nature of postwar Europe. On July 18, Churchill asked his colleagues what exactly

---

[31] Truman to Bess Truman, July 20, 1945, in Ferrell, ed., *Dear Bess*, p. 520.
[32] Brown diary, July 20, 1945, Byrnes Papers, Folder 54 (1).
[33] Robertson, *Sly and Able*, pp. 420–421.
[34] Stalin quoted in Walter Brown diary on Potsdam, July 17, 1945, Byrnes Papers, Folder 54 (1).

PHOTO 6. Triple handshake! President Truman held Winston Churchill's and Josef Stalin's hands in a triple handshake during the opening day of the Potsdam Conference. The occasion was a dinner given by Churchill at his residence for Truman and Stalin on July 17, 1945. (Courtesy National Archives.)

constituted Germany and this broke open the dispute over German boundaries. Because the Soviets gouged such a large portion of prewar Poland in the east they wished to "compensate" Poland in the west at German expense. Prior to Yalta the Soviets suggested the Oder River as the new Polish-German border. By Yalta their demands had escalated so that they proposed that the border should run along the Oder and western Neisse Rivers, thereby providing an additional 8,000 square miles to postwar Poland, an area, so they later clarified, from which no reparations might be drawn. Roosevelt and Churchill balked at this request at Yalta and Churchill and Truman initially did the same at Potsdam.[35] Stalin, in turn, balked at the American proposals to retreat from specific dollar allocations for reparations, and he tried to retain the monetary sum of ten billion dollars as the Soviet share. The procedures for governing occupied Germany and especially control arrangements for the industrial Ruhr area also put the Soviets and the western allies at odds. So too did the issues of recognition of the Soviet dominated regimes in Bulgaria, Rumania, and Hungary and, inevitably, the application of the Declaration on Liberated Europe to the people of Poland.

By the time Churchill, Attlee, and Eden left Potsdam to return to London to hear the delayed British elections results, the conference discussions had bogged down on major issues. Churchill had taken on Stalin on a number of issues with true British bulldog spirit. He negated Stalin's proposal to overthrow Franco's regime, criticized Tito's behavior in Yugoslavia, demanded access from Stalin to the assigned western zones in Austria, sidetracked the Soviet interest in the Italian colonies, clashed with Stalin over his proposal to establish a Russian military base in the Dardanelles, and vigorously opposed the Soviet proposal on the German-Poland border.[36] From the British perspective he had kept "his end up," despite Truman's "not giving him much support."[37] Truman had not tried to play the role of mediator or honest broker between the British and the Russians that some British officials had predicted on the eve of the conference, but he continued to hope and work for viable agreements so he could return home from what he described as "this terrible place."[38] He had his disagreements with Stalin at the conference table but, with Davies as his constant monitor, he continued to assure the Soviet leader of his genuine hopes for peace. He pushed for reorganization of the satellite governments under Soviet control but never with the gusto of Churchill, and he never pressed with the force of the British prime minister for the quick holding of the promised elections in Poland. His main concerns remained to secure

---

[35] Truman wrote Bess on July 25 that "Russia and Poland have gobbled up a big hunk of Germany and want Britain and us to agree. I have flatly refused." Ferrell, ed., *Dear Bess*, p. 521.

[36] Gilbert provides a good summary in his *Winston S. Churchill*, Vol. VIII (Boston, 1988) pp. 78–91.

[37] The judgment of Admiral Sir Andrew Cunningham quoted in Gilbert, *Winston S. Churchill*, VIII, p. 89.

[38] For Truman's description of Potsdam see Ferrell, ed., *Off the Record*, p. 54.

the quick end to the Pacific War and to make sure that the United States avoided subsidizing the peace settlement.

Soviet behavior at the conference and beyond it troubled Secretary Byrnes much more than it did the president. On July 24, the day before Churchill departed, Byrnes confided to Walter Brown that "somebody had made an awful mistake in bringing about a situation where Russia was permitted to come out of a war with the power she will have." Rather ironically Byrnes did not assign any culpability to the United States and didn't reflect on what might have been done differently at the Yalta conference, or even earlier by the Americans. No, the culprit in the Byrnes analysis turned out to be England, which he opined, "should never have permitted Hitler to rise" because "the German people under a democracy would have been a far superior ally than Russia." Moving beyond Byrnes's excursion into the wisdom of hindsight, it was clear that he recognized that the collapse of German power allowed the Russians to extend their sphere of power far into Europe. Now he worried increasingly about how to arrest this Soviet expansion. He feared that maintaining a "long-time program of co-operation" with the Soviets would be difficult given their ideological differences with the United States and the United Kingdom.[39] At last the proverbial penny was beginning to drop for Byrnes.

Such legitimate and well-grounded fears did not paralyze the pragmatic Byrnes. He played the hand he had been dealt and proceeded forward to gain the best arrangements and settlements he could. Also he had other matters demanding his and the president's attention, especially the matter of forcing Japan's surrender. With the powerful destructive force of the atomic bomb fully confirmed by subsequent reports after July 17, the United States prepared to issue a final warning to the Japanese. Stimson still sought to amend the surrender terms specifically to allow for a guarantee for the Japanese to retain their emperor, but Truman and Byrnes with Churchill's eventual agreement held to the unconditional surrender demand. Thus, on July 26, the very day Churchill resigned his commission as prime minister, the leaders of the United States and the United Kingdom (with the further endorsement of the Chinese) issued the Potsdam declaration. It warned the Japanese to surrender immediately or to face "prompt and utter destruction." The declaration denied any intention "that the Japanese shall be enslaved as a race or destroyed as a nation," but promised that "stern justice shall be meted out to all war criminals." It pledged that Allied occupation forces eventually would be withdrawn as soon as

[39] Diary entry, July 24, 1945, Brown Diary, Byrnes Papers, Folder 602.

"there has been established in accordance with the freely expressed will of the Japanese people a peacefully inclined and responsible government." The Potsdam statement did not mention the emperor, but called for the unconditional surrender of "all Japanese armed forces."[40]

Two days prior to the issuance of the Potsdam Declaration, Truman sidled over to Stalin at the conclusion of the July 24 plenary session and advised him that the United States had developed a "new weapon of unusual destructive force." He gave no specific information on the atomic bomb, and, of course, Stalin hardly needed any given his own sources on the bomb including the spy Klaus Fuchs who was at Alamogordo at the time of the Trinity test. According to Truman's account Stalin responded that "he was glad to hear it and hoped we would make 'good use of it against the Japanese.'"[41] Anthony Eden standing close by thought Stalin merely nodded and said: "thank you."[42] However this may be, Truman made no effort to clarify for Stalin the extent and power of the new weapon.[43] One might have thought that if the president aimed to take advantage of the diplomatic potential of the atomic weapon then he might have played up the power of the new weapon to the full, allowing the Soviets to understand that the United States held this new force in its arsenal – a weapon that obviated the need for any Soviet support in the Pacific War. Of course he did no such thing, because he had no intention or desire to engage in any such explicit diplomacy.

Truman's attention focused instead on the use of "the most terrible bomb in the history of the world" against Japan. While he mused privately that the bomb might be "the fire distruction (sic) prophesied in the Euphrates Valley Era after Noah and his fabulous Ark," his interest centered on forcing Japan's defeat. On the eve of the Potsdam Declaration he noted in his diary: "I have told Sec. Of War, Mr. Stimson, to use it so that military objectives and soldiers and sailors are the target and not women and children." Indicative of his attitude toward the Japanese, he continued, "even if the Japs are savages, ruthless, merciless and fanatic, we as the leader of the world for the common welfare cannot drop this terrible bomb on the

---

[40] "Proclamation Defining Terms for Japanese Surrender" (Potsdam Declaration), July 26, 1945, *Department of State Bulletin*, Vol. 13 (July 29, 1945), pp. 137–138.

[41] Truman, *Year of Decisions*, p. 458.

[42] Anthony Eden, *The Reckoning: The Eden Memoirs* (Boston, 1965) p. 635.

[43] See David Holloway, "The Atomic Bomb and the End of the Wartime Alliance," in Ann Lane and Howard Temperley, eds., *The Rise and Fall of the Grand Alliance, 1941–45* (New York, 1995), pp. 211–212. For further details see Holloway's *Stalin and the Bomb: The Soviet Union and Atomic Energy, 1939–1956* (New Haven, CT, 1994), pp. 115–133.

old capital [Kyoto] or the new [Tokyo]." Truman also held that "we will issue a warning statement asking the Japs to surrender and save lives. I'm sure they will not do that, but we will have given them the chance."[44] Undoubtedly, as Barton Bernstein has noted, this comment reveals "what can only be regarded as self-deception," on Truman's part regarding the number of noncombatants who would be killed by the atomic bomb.[45] But the American president clearly focused more on saving American lives than on likely Japanese casualties.

Byrnes attempted his own limited exercise in diplomacy influenced by the American possession of the atomic bomb, although without any explicit approval from Truman. On July 23 he explained his effort to Churchill. The secretary of state had cabled Chinese Foreign Minister T. V. Soong and encouraged him not to make any further concessions to the Soviets on the Sino-Soviet agreement foreshadowed at Yalta. He encouraged Soong to keep on negotiating, hoping that the Soviet Union would delay its entry into the war until agreements were finalized. Byrnes also explained his thinking to Walter Brown who recorded on July 24 that "JFB still hoping for time, believing after atomic bomb Japan will surrender and Russia will not get in so much on the kill." Byrnes further shared his hopes with Navy Secretary James Forrestal on July 26 and told him he "was most anxious to get the Japanese affair over with before the Russians got in, with particular reference to Dairen and Port Arthur." As Byrnes understood well: "Once in there, he felt it would not be easy to get them out."[46] In retrospect, Byrnes's attempt to limit and restrict Soviet encroachment in the northeast Asian region is admirable and speaks to his developing grasp of international realities, but his effort failed. From the outset it more resembled wishful thinking than a serious diplomatic initiative. As Byrnes eventually understood, nothing the United States might do could keep the Soviets out of the war. They simply possessed the military force to have their way in Manchuria and north China. The secretary of state regretfully accepted this reality, and thus, noted David Robertson correctly, "ended Jimmy Byrnes' brief flirtation with atomic diplomacy."[47] Or, at least it did for the time being, and Byrnes turned back to concentrate on the conference deliberations.

---

[44] Diary entry, July 25, 1945, in Ferrell, ed., *Off the Record*, p. 55.
[45] See Barton J. Bernstein, "Understanding the Atomic Bomb and the Japanese Surrender: Missed Opportunities, Little-Known Near Disasters, and Modern Memory," *Diplomatic History*, Vol. 19 (Spring, 1995), pp. 257–258.
[46] Millis, ed., *The Forrestal Diaries*, p. 78.   [47] Robertson, *Sly and Able*, p. 422.

Much to the surprise of the American delegation the British voters sent a new prime minister and a new foreign secretary back to Potsdam on July 27. Churchill had expected victory on the strength of his great wartime leadership but the British electorate concentrated on domestic concerns and looked forward rather than backward. The political tide ran against the Tories in favor of Clement Attlee's Labour Party. Churchill feared that his successors might not be up to the task that lay ahead for them, but his questioning of the competence of the Labour leaders proved ill-founded. Attlee and, more notably, his foreign secretary Ernest Bevin eventually emerged as key contributors to the Western response to the Soviet Union. Whatever the differing visions of Labour and the Conservatives in the British domestic realm, the emergence of a new government brought about no major departures in British foreign policy. Attlee and Bevin returned to Potsdam working essentially from the same policy briefs.

The British leaders, who returned to the Potsdam conference table on July 28, found that negotiations were moving ahead rapidly to forge a compromise settlement on the major disputed issues. Byrnes seized the initiative. He already had planted some seeds prior to the departure of Churchill when he proposed to Eden and Molotov on July 24 that "as something like 50% of the goods available for reparation are in the Russian zone and as Russia claims 50% of reparations, Russia should take what it likes from her own zone." Further, he suggested that "the other zone commanders should make what deliveries they decide to make each from their own zones to the other countries entitled to reparations so as to satisfy their shares." Molotov had responded cautiously by offering that he would consider the idea so long as the Soviet Union might obtain additional "deliveries worth $3 billion from the Ruhr," an amount Byrnes would not countenance.[48] The reparations issue, like the Polish-German boundary, remained as seemingly impossible hurdles for the conferees to jump.

Into this stalemate stepped the irrepressible and inevitably fretting Joseph Davies. On July 28 he met with Byrnes and listened as the secretary shared his view that the news of the atomic bomb might gain some diplomatic leverage with the Russians. Davies challenged that notion immediately arguing that any "threat of exclusion from participation in this new war weapon" would only create distrust and cause the Soviets to get their backs up. He offered a different strategy. He now suggested the

---

[48] See Eden's minutes of the meeting, July 24, 1945, Avon Papers, Main Library Special Collections, University of Birmingham, Folder 20/13/236.

time had arrived "to get down to a little 'horseback (sic) trading.'" In his view nothing more could be gained by "talk." Instead, he posited, "might it not be a good thing to tie up Reparations, the Satellite States, the Polish Border and Italy together in a package proposal and try to get an end to debate and secure an agreement through simultaneous concessions, and dispose of them together?" Byrnes replied, according to Davies's account, "I think you've got something there."[49] He certainly meant what he said and proceeded to act on the Davies suggestion.

Over a series of meetings from July 29 to July 31 the negotiators forged the main outline of a compromise.[50] Byrnes gave ground on the cession of German territory to Poland and gave some limited promise of recognition to the Soviet-sponsored regimes in Rumania, Hungary, and Bulgaria. In turn, he put pressure on Molotov to concede on the reparations issue and forego any reference to fixed dollar amounts of payments. Furthermore, the Russians would be assigned no involvement in the Ruhr. Molotov objected in one meeting to Byrnes's reneging on the Yalta reparations accord, but Byrnes met his complaint by indicating that circumstances had changed. The level of destruction in Germany was greater than expected and also the Soviets unilaterally had consigned to Poland a much larger portion of Germany than that expected at Yalta. On the morning of July 31 according to Byrnes's account the secretary of state met with his Soviet counterpart, explicitly linked the three issues, and asked him to present his proposal to Stalin. Byrnes put the issue bluntly. "I told him," he recalled, "we would agree to all three or none and that the President and I would leave for the United States the next day."[51] It represented a "package deal, take it or leave it," as Charles Mee noted.[52]

At the plenary session later in the afternoon of July 31 Stalin joined Attlee and Truman at the conference table. At Truman's request Byrnes set forth his proposal and Stalin tried to chip away at the terms set forth. The Americans refused to budge further and Stalin faced the reality that he now dealt with a genuine *quid pro quo* approach. He decided to accept the deal that Byrnes offered. With Soviet agreement on the compromise the settlements flowed quickly – reparations, the German-Polish boundary, limited recognition for the East European governments. Other issues such as the

---

[49] Davies Journal, July 28, 1945, Davies Papers, Box 19. (One assumes that Davies meant "horse-trading" rather than "horseback-trading"!)

[50] The various meetings are tracked quite well in Mee, *Meeting at Potsdam*, pp. 255–268.

[51] Byrnes, *Speaking Frankly*, pp. 84–85.   [52] Mee, *Meeting at Potsdam*, p. 262.

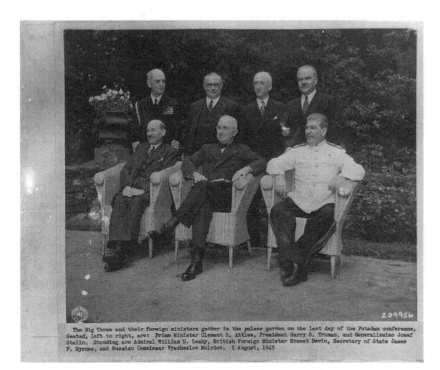

The Big Three and their foreign ministers gather in the palace garden on the last day of the Potsdam conference, Seated, left to right, are: Prime Minister Clement R. Attlee, President Harry S. Truman, and Generalissimo Josef Stalin. Standing are Admiral William D. Leahy, British Foreign Minister Ernest Bevin, Secretary of State James F. Byrnes, and Russian Commissar Vyacheslav Molotov, 1 August, 1945

PHOTO 7. The Big Three – Prime Minister Clement R. Attlee, President Harry S. Truman, and Generalissimo Josef Stalin – and their foreign ministers, along with Admiral Leahy, gather in the palace garden on the last day of the Potsdam Conference, August 1, 1945. (Courtesy National Archives.)

treatment of war criminals were settled quickly and incorporated into the Potsdam protocol.[53] A Big Three agreement emerged.

Late in the evening of August 1, at an hour when Truman normally would be awake only if playing poker and drinking bourbon, the leaders of the Big Three gathered for the final plenary session. Drafts of the final communiqué and of the Potsdam accords lay before the principals and they worked their way through them section by section. Eventually the president, the generalissimo, and the prime minister signed the accords. Truman, the neophyte diplomat, then abruptly declared the Berlin Conference adjourned, observing that he hoped the next meeting would be in Washington. Stalin, a former seminarian unused to invoking the Almighty, replied: "God willing." After further pleasantries, the delegates exchanged handshakes, extended good wishes for safe travel, and then

[53] Protocol of proceedings, August 1, 1945, *FRUS: Potsdam, 1945*, II, pp. 1477–1498.

dispersed. By 8:00 A.M. Truman's plane departed Berlin to return him to the United States. His first – and last – major exercise in international summitry had ended. He would never see Stalin again.

Both Truman and Byrnes judged Potsdam a success of sorts. Byrnes recalled that "the conference ended in good spirits," although he admitted that the returning delegation from Berlin "probably was less sanguine than the one that had departed from Yalta." The ill-based optimism of the Yalta gathering had been tempered by the subsequent months of difficulties and disagreements among the Allies. And, the hard bargaining at Potsdam seemed to indicate that there would be no easy resolution of divisive issues. Nonetheless, Byrnes thought that "a basis for maintaining our war-born unity" had been established at the conference. He believed that the Potsdam agreements "would provide a basis for the early restoration of stability in Europe." Writing in 1947 in his memoir *Speaking Frankly* Byrnes held that "the agreements did make the conference a success but the violation of those agreements has turned success into failure." Potsdam, he maintained, was "the success that failed."[54] Truman shared this outlook. Like Byrnes he saw the difficulty of Potsdam in the failure of the Soviets to abide by the agreements negotiated there. In 1957 he referred to the large number of agreements that were reached there – "only to be broken as soon as the unconscionable Russian Dictator returned to Moscow."[55]

Truman certainly presented the Potsdam results as a success in the report he gave to the American people on his return. He enjoined his fellow citizens to use "all our resources and all our skills in the great cause of a just and lasting peace" and gave a final assurance that "the three great powers are now more closely than ever bound together in determination to achieve that kind of peace." Linking himself again with FDR he proclaimed: "From Tehran, and the Crimea, and San Francisco, and Berlin – we shall continue to march together to our objective."[56] Yet his presentation of the result of the American labors at Potsdam had a certain disingenuous quality about it. For the most part what he said reasonably reflected the details of the accords, but he failed to make clear that, guided by his new secretary of state, he had moved in the direction of forging a sphere of influence peace. Although Truman, in the usual pious American fashion, even included a line in his statement reaffirming that the East European

[54] Byrnes, *Speaking Frankly*, pp. 86–87.

[55] Truman (unsent letter) to Acheson, March 15, 1957, in Monte M. Poen, ed., *Strictly Personal and Confidential: The Letters Harry S. Truman Never Mailed* (Boston, 1982), p. 33.

[56] Report of the President on the Berlin Conference, August 9, 1945, *Department of State Bulletin*, Vol. 13 (August 12, 1945), pp. 208–213.

nations were not to be included in the "spheres of influence of any one power," the Potsdam deliberations belie his stance.[57] This whole matter has not always been well appreciated even by some of the most astute of observers, including Henry Kissinger, who branded Potsdam "a dialogue of the deaf" that "accomplished little."[58] Such views ignore the underlying rationale and the ramifications of the deal that Byrnes negotiated at Potsdam. These views disregard that Byrnes and Truman laid the foundations at Potsdam for what they hoped would be a workable postwar settlement with the Soviet Union.[59]

Byrnes had kept Truman fully briefed as he negotiated the outlines of the final settlement with Molotov. The president readily accepted Byrnes's proposal as a way to break the impasse that beset the conference and which kept him trapped in Germany for over two weeks. He did not see the Potsdam deal as constituting a major break with the policies of his predecessor. While it clearly marked a retreat from some of the specific terms of the Yalta accord, especially regarding reparations matters and the economic administration of Germany, he felt the arrangements forged would secure continued cooperation between the United States and the Soviet Union. Like his predecessor Truman accepted that the Soviets would dominate in the part of Europe their army occupied. In a conversation with James Forrestal on July 28 he blamed Hitler for the reality that "we shall have a Slav Europe for a long time to come," but then he added rather nonchalantly in words that would have troubled all genuine East European democrats, "I don't think it is so bad."[60] Clearly he had no idea what lay ahead for those who would contest Soviet (Slav) domination.

It is crucial to appreciate that the American policy makers virtually backed into this arrangement in order to obtain agreements with the Soviets at Potsdam. This was not the deliberate formulation and execution of a grand strategy, but tactical policy making on the run. Truman and Byrnes had not arrived at Potsdam set upon negotiating a "spheres of influence" peace. However, the firm American resolve not to subsidize German reparations either directly or indirectly, along with a concern to lay some foundation for economic and social stability in postwar Europe,

---

[57] Truman's report on Berlin Conference, August 9, 1945, *Department of State Bulletin*, Vol. 13 (August 12, 1945), p. 211.

[58] See Henry Kissinger, *Diplomacy* (New York, 1994), pp. 330–331.

[59] The insightful work of Marc Trachtenberg has been crucial to guiding my own thinking on this subject. See his *A Constructed Peace*, pp. 22–33.

[60] Diary extract for July 28, 1945, Forrestal Diaries, Vol. 2, Forrestal Papers, Mudd Library, Princeton University, Princeton, NJ.

had prompted them to settle on the arrangement whereby each occupying power would take reparations from its own zone. This arrangement, however, had significant strategic ramifications for the broader postwar settlement. Although it evolved out of a sincere desire to forge a settlement with the Soviets and to limit the grounds for future disputes, it moved significantly in the direction of dividing Germany.

The irony in the American approach needs to be emphasized. Byrnes and Truman wanted to reach a genuine settlement with the Soviet Union and to maintain a decent, cooperative relationship with their wartime ally into the postwar years. Yet, in order to do that and to meet their own key objective regarding reparations, they had to limit the extent of their cooperation with the Soviets. Marc Trachtenberg captures Byrnes's underlying sentiment well in arguing that for the western allies and the Soviets, "the way to get along was to pull apart" and to reach an "amicable understanding."[61] Truman and Byrnes arrived at Potsdam intent on following FDR and so to continuing decent relations with the Soviet Union, but they operated as politicians who would make adjustments to forge a decent settlement. Byrnes once compared the Soviets to the U.S. Senate: "You build a post office in their state, and they'll build a post office in our state."[62] At Potsdam he operated out of this perspective.

Of course the Potsdam settlement did not end contact between the Soviets and the Americans. Indeed, the allied powers through the Potsdam agreements locked themselves into certain institutional structures to continue their cooperation both through the Council of Foreign Ministers and through the Allied Control Council to oversee broadly the German occupation. Truman and Byrnes left Germany hopeful that the compromise reached there would afford good relations with Soviets. Truman gladly deputized Byrnes to continue the deliberations that would wrap up all the details and ready the way for the final peace conference which he expected to attend with Stalin and Attlee. There had been no reversal on his part of the effort by his predecessor to work cooperatively with Stalin.

Nonetheless, Potsdam provided the location for some movement away from the accommodating approach of Roosevelt. Byrnes led it, and Truman followed him. Byrnes began to appreciate the real danger that the expansion of Soviet power represented in both Europe and in northeast Asia. He tried without success to prevent expansion in the latter region but eventually recognized that Soviet movement into Manchuria and Korea

---

[61] Trachtenberg, *A Constructed Peace*, pp. 27, 28.
[62] Quoted in Larson, *Origins of Containment*, p. 194.

was a fait accompli. Even if the Soviets were not needed to defeat the Japanese nothing could prevent them from rushing in to grab some share of the spoils of victory. In Europe Byrnes implicitly drew a limit on further Soviet advances. Perhaps he didn't fully appreciate all the implications himself but by forcing the reparations settlement on Stalin he limited significantly the opportunity for the Soviet Union to meddle in the western half of Germany. Given that Stalin hoped to impose a "Soviet-style anti-fascist democracy (sic)" on postwar Germany and that his ambitions certainly extended well beyond the German lands occupied by his brutal army, Byrnes's initiative must be acknowledged as crucial in the postwar effort to secure Western Europe.[63] Byrnes, at least, began at Potsdam to appreciate that "the most likely future threat to the nation's security was the Kremlin's potential to gain preponderance in Western Europe through the success of Communist parties or by maneuvering to gain control of all of Germany."[64] The American effort at Potsdam placed some real obstacles in the way of Soviet ambitions beyond their sphere.

Truman and Byrnes hurried back across the Atlantic as soon as the Potsdam Conference concluded. One might have thought the president would take advantage of his proximity to London to visit the capital of his nation's closest wartime ally and to pay tribute to its courageous citizens. But time was of the essence so he allowed a quick shipboard visit with Britain's head of state, King George VI, to suffice. Truman wanted to get home. He and Byrnes appeared to spend little time debriefing on the Potsdam meeting and taking the measure of the Soviet leader they dealt with there. Their focus now rested on the future and bringing the war with Japan to a successful end. They received further reports of Japanese peace feelers and worried that Japan might seek to surrender through the Soviet Union rather than some neutral country like Sweden. Most of all they waited for news of the atomic bomb. On August 3, the president and his secretary of state good-naturedly chided Admiral Leahy "not to hold out news on the atomic bomb."[65] The old admiral, trained in another age, still expressed doubts about the military impact of the bomb and his negativity about the weapon was well known. Before the USS *Augusta* reached its American port, however, Admiral Leahy had been shown to be quite wrong. Hiroshima had been bombed.

---

[63] On Soviet ambitions in Germany see R. C. Raack, *Stalin's Drive to the West, 1938–1945: The Origins of the Cold War* (Stanford, 1995), pp. 112–213.

[64] Melvyn P. Leffler, *The Struggle for Germany and the Origins of the Cold War* (Washington, D.C., 1996), p. 24.

[65] Brown diary, August 3, 1945, Byrnes Papers, Folder 602.

CHAPTER 5

Hiroshima, the Japanese, and the Soviets

The final orders to use the atomic bombs had been issued well before Truman began his journey home from Potsdam. On July 25 General Marshall's deputy, Gen. Thomas Handy, serving as the acting chief of staff, wrote at the direction of Stimson and Marshall to Gen. Carl Spaatz, the commanding general of the Army Strategic Air Forces and told him: "The 509 Composite Group, 20th Air Force will deliver its first special bomb as soon as weather will permit visual bombing after about 3 August 1945 on one of the targets: Hiroshima, Kokura, Niigata and Nagasaki." Handy went further and instructed that "additional bombs will be delivered on the above targets as soon as ready by the project staff," and he explained that "further instructions will be issued concerning targets other than those listed above."[1] Notably, there was no suggestion here that only two bombs would be used. The American military prepared to utilize the atomic weapons as they became available.

Stimson had alerted Truman on July 30 of the rapid progress on what he termed "Groves's" project and the expected use of the atomic bomb in early August. The secretary of war also obtained Truman's approval for the White House to release a prepared statement once the bomb had been delivered on its target. It must be appreciated that the American military largely controlled the specific timing of the bomb's use and Truman proved quite content to delegate that responsibility. Indeed, Truman possessed few hesitations about using the weapon, and he simply wanted the military planning to reach fruition. Whatever the subsequent controversies over the

---

[1] Handy Directive to Spaatz, July 25, 1945, in Kort, ed., *The Columbia Guide to Hiroshima and the Bomb*, p. 259.

atomic bomb, this decision caused him none of the anxiety that afflicted him during later difficult decisions, such as when he fired Douglas MacArthur in 1951 in the midst of the Korean War. It constituted an important but hardly a "controversial" decision for him.

Notably, no action of the Japanese government or military in the period after the Potsdam Declaration encouraged either Truman or Byrnes to consider any change in American strategy. Quite the opposite! Having broken the Japanese codes the Americans knew of the tentative, back-channel efforts of certain civilian officials in Tokyo to enlist the Soviet Union in negotiating some kind of peace settlement that would *not* require either a surrender and occupation of the home islands or any fundamental changes in the Japanese imperial system (*kokutai*).[2] But such terms were completely unacceptable to the Allies. The American-led alliance intended "unrestricted occupation of Japanese territory, total authority in the governing of Japan, dismantlement of Japan's military and military-industrial complex ('demobilization'), a restructuring of Japanese society ('demilitarization'), and Allied-run war crimes trials."[3] Japan must concede fully as had Germany. No indication of such a surrender occurred, of course, because the influential Japanese decision makers could not countenance it.[4] So the American policy makers waited in vain for the Japanese to respond positively to the Potsdam Declaration's call for immediate and unconditional surrender. Instead, Japan's Prime Minister Suzuki Kantaro publicly dismissed the Potsdam terms on July 28 and on July 30. When referring to the terms, he confided to a senior cabinet official that "for the enemy to say something like that means circumstances have arisen that force them also to end the war. That is why they are talking about unconditional surrender. Precisely at a time like this, if we hold firm, then they will yield before we do." He did not "think there is any need to stop [the war.]"[5]

In the post-Potsdam period the Tokyo government held back from any official contact with the Allies through the formal channels provided by the

---

[2] See the collection of Japanese diplomatic cables from July 2 to August 16 to which Byrnes had access in Byrnes Papers, Folder 571. On the limits of Japan's negotiating terms as revealed in these diplomatic exchanges see Frank, *Downfall*, pp. 229–230.

[3] These terms are set forth in Douglas J. MacEachin, *The Final Months of the War With Japan*, p. 36.

[4] For brilliant expositions of the Japanese determination throughout 1945 to continue fighting see Richard B. Frank's, *Downfall*, esp. pp. 83–86; and Herbert P. Bix, "Japan's Delayed Surrender: A Reinterpretation," *Diplomatic History*, Vol. 19 (Spring, 1995), pp. 197–225.

[5] Suzuki quoted in Bix, "Japan's Delayed Surrender," p. 208.

Swiss government. Despite the thunderous bombing campaign of General Curtis LeMay's B-29s from March to August, which had left no sizable city untouched, the Japanese planned to continue their war effort.[6] Indeed, members of the Japanese military appeared to relish the opportunity to punish American invaders who dared intrude on their home islands.[7] They held to the main elements of the *Ketsu-Go* ("Decisive Operation") strategy designed to crush the expected American invaders such that the American population would grow weary of the conflict and agree to terms. American officials fully appreciated this as the excellent research of the military historians Edward Drea and D. M. Giangreco has now made indisputably clear.[8]

Late in July American intelligence utilizing the ULTRA code-breaking system determined that the Japanese troop levels in Kyushu dedicated to repelling any invasion had grown by six divisions over June and July and even more soldiers were arriving. General MacArthur's intelligence chief, Maj. Gen. Charles Willoughby, even expressed the fear that Japanese forces could "grow to [the] point where we attack on a ratio of one (1) to one (1)," which, he helpfully added for even the most obtuse of his readers, "is not the recipe for victory."[9] The prospects for the Olympic invasion now appeared decidedly problematic and the likelihood of significant American casualties commensurately increased. "The odds were against the invaders," as Drea explained, "because the defenders would soon equal or outnumber the attackers on the beaches." On the day of the American attack on Hiroshima, estimates held that the Japanese Army "now had 600,000 troops in Kyushu and expected even more."[10] The commanders of these determined troops expected the support of over four thousand *kamikaze* planes along with conventional fighter aircraft and torpedo planes whose combined attacks might knock out fifteen to twenty percent of the invasion force (three entire divisions) while still at sea.[11] In such circumstances none of the American military leaders either in

---

[6] For a vivid portrayal of the bombing campaign see Ronald Schaffer, *Wings of Judgment: American Bombing in World War II* (New York, 1985), pp. 128–142.

[7] Frank, *Downfall*, pp. 83–86.

[8] Giangreco provides the most detailed and penetrating analysis of Japanese defensive preparations in his brilliantly researched *Hell to Pay*.

[9] This analysis relies upon, and Willoughby's evaluation is quoted in, Frank, *Downfall*, pp. 211–212.

[10] Edward J. Drea, *In the Service of the Emperor Essays on the Japanese Army* (Lincoln, NE, 1998), pp. 161, 164. The following sentences also rely in part on Drea's valuable research.

[11] On the strength of the Japanese Imperial Army and Navy air forces see Giangreco, *Hell to Pay*, p. 78.

the Pacific theater or in Washington cautioned Truman to reconsider his use of the atomic bomb. The reality was quite the opposite. Apprised of the bloody carnage that awaited his invading force General Marshall even asked Leslie Groves in late July about the feasibility of using atomic bombs as tactical weapons to diminish the Japanese resistance on Kyushu![12]

The on-the-ground reality of a Japanese military "girding for Armageddon" and convinced "that it could achieve success against an invasion," must be well appreciated by all who genuinely seek to understand why the atomic bombs were used.[13] In short, Japan hardly stood on the verge of military defeat. The time has come at long last to explode permanently the myth of a Japan ready to surrender – a notion that received much of its currency from the terribly flawed report of the United States Strategic Bombing Survey conducted after the war and publicly issued in July of 1946.[14] This view has done enough damage to proper understanding of the use of the atomic bomb.

While the Japanese readied themselves for the climactic battle for their home islands, feverish preparations continued on Tinian, a tiny island in the Marianas chain. Here the flight and ordnance crews under the respective commands of Col. Paul W. Tibbets, Jr., and Capt. William S. ("Deak") Parsons made their final preparations to use the new atomic weapon in warfare. Tinian lay 1,500 miles south of Japan and had been captured in July 1944 after characteristically vicious fighting. Once secured, the U.S. construction battalions set about transforming the island into what Stephen Walker rightly described as the "biggest air base in the world." They hurriedly built six huge runways there and soon LeMay's B-29s were flying off them to attack targets in Japan. All the various bomber groups based on the island joined to form a "machine of mass destruction" through the early months of 1945 except for the 509th Composite Group commanded by Colonel Tibbets.[15] This

---

[12] Drea, *In the Service of the Emperor*, pp. 163–164.

[13] These descriptions of the Japanese military are from Frank, *Downfall*, p. 238.

[14] On the serious flaws of the U.S. Strategic Bombing Survey see Robert P. Newman, "Ending the War with Japan: Paul Nitze's 'Early Surrender' Counterfactual," *Pacific Historical Review*, Vol. 64 (May, 1995), pp. 167–194; and Barton J. Bernstein, "Compelling Japan's Surrender without the A-bomb, Soviet Entry, or Invasion: Reconsidering the US Bombing Survey's Early Surrender Conclusions," *Journal of Strategic Studies*, Vol. 18 (June, 1995), pp. 101–148. Bernstein noted that "analysts can no longer trust the Survey's statements of counterfactual probabilities about when the Pacific War would have ended without the A-Bomb or Soviet entry. On such matters, the Survey is an unreliable guide" (p. 105).

[15] The details here and the direct quotations are from Stephen Walker, *Shockwave: Countdown to Hiroshima* (New York, 2005), pp. 82–85.

PHOTO 8. Little Boy, the atomic bomb that destroyed Hiroshima. (Courtesy Harry S. Truman Presidential Library.)

specially trained group flying distinctive B-29s modified to carry especially large bombs held back from any bombing assignments over Japan. But, by early August their time to fly to the Japanese home islands had come.

Paul Tibbets's father had pressured him to study medicine, but with his mother's backing he instead decided to fly airplanes. He proved an excellent pilot and distinguished himself flying B-17 bombers over Nazi-occupied Europe in 1942. His superb flying skills earned him the command of the team charged with dropping the atomic bombs. He "assembled a team of experienced flyers," as Michael Gordin records, "and managed to prepare them quickly and with discipline under exceptional circumstances."[16] Tibbets oversaw fifteen special atomic bombers and he commanded fifteen crews trained to fly them. There is little indication that Tibbets and his superiors expected one or even two bombs to suffice to force a Japanese capitulation. Tibbets recalled soon after the war that "I thought it would take five atom bombs to jar the

[16] Gordin, *Five Days in August*, p. 77.

PHOTO 9. The *Enola Gay* sitting on an airfield circa 1945 with signatures of its crew, including Paul Tibbets. (Courtesy Harry S. Truman Presidential Library.)

Japanese into quitting," but it is clear that as of early August he planned to deliver effectively whatever number came to him.[17]

Deak Parsons is not as well known as Tibbets in the accounts of the bombing of Hiroshima, but he played a similarly crucial role. Parsons had a far longer association with the atomic bomb than the experienced pilot. An accomplished ballistics expert, he had been drawn into the Manhattan Project by Groves and Oppenheimer and played an important part in "the development of the bomb as a droppable, deliverable weapon."[18] He had observed the first atomic explosion at Alamogordo from a B-29 observation plane far above the desert. He then left for Tinian and bore the on site responsibility for assembling the atomic weapons. By August 1 he had completed his crucial work, although he spent subsequent days rehearsing endlessly the difficult and painful steps he would undertake to activate the bomb in flight. (Parsons feared an atomic explosion if the B-29 carrying it

[17] Tibbets quoted in Gordin, *Five Days in August*, p. 83.
[18] On Parsons see Walker, *Shockwave*, p. 61.

were to crash on take-off, so he decided that he must ready the bomb on the mission to deliver it.) The "Little Boy" bomb remained in the bomb assembly building for some further days, however, as the aircrews waited for favorable weather reports. Clear skies were predicted for August 6.

On August 5 Tibbets decided to name the strike plane he had chosen to fly in honor of the mother who had supported his decision to become a pilot. Late in the afternoon he instructed a sign painter to apply eight letters underneath the cockpit. So it was that his plane carried the name *Enola Gay* on the most famous and controversial air mission ever.[19] Tibbets never expressed regret about associating his mother with his deadly undertaking. He always held to the view that he engaged in a military strike to force an end to the war. But such future controversies were far from his mind during the evening of August 5. The final briefings were completed and during that evening the loading crew hoisted "Little Boy" into the bomb bay of the *Enola Gay*.

Early in the morning of August 6 the crews of Tibbets's plane and those of the accompanying weather and observer planes heard their chaplain pray to God that "armed with Thy strength may they bring this war to a rapid end." At 2:45 A.M. (Tinian time) Tibbets took off and flew toward Japan. Once the *Enola Gay* reached its steady flying altitude Parsons entered the bomb bay and made the final adjustments to the bomb to allow for its eventual detonation. Guided by the reports of the weather reconnaissance plane, Tibbets concluded that they should attack their primary target. Around 8:15 A.M. (Japanese time, which was 7:15 P.M. August 5 in Washington, D.C.) the *Enola Gay* dropped its solitary weapon on the city of Hiroshima.[20]

Harry Truman's seaboard journey back across the Atlantic on the USS *Augusta* had given him time to relax, and it included a similar complement of movies and musical concerts for evening entertainment as had his journey to Potsdam. Enjoying the calm seas, he continued his regular practice of rising early and getting in a good walk on deck before breakfast. He consulted occasionally with Secretary Byrnes, Admiral Leahy, and White House Counsel Samuel Rosenman on the report he would offer the American people on the Potsdam meeting. And, of course, with assistance from his naval and military aides, Captain James Vardaman and Brigadier General Harry Vaughan, he monitored developments from the

---

[19] This relies on Walker, *Shockwave*, pp. 193–194.
[20] This summary account draws primarily from Weintraub, *The Last Great Victory*, pp. 413–418. (For the chaplain's prayer see p. 415.)

Pacific battlefronts. These developments held both positive and tragic news for the American president eager to bring the bloody war to an end. While the American air force and navy continued their relentless efforts to pound the Japanese into submission, the costs in American lives continued to mount. The sinking of the cruiser USS *Indianapolis* – the very ship that had delivered the key components of the atomic bombs to Tinian Island – by a Japanese submarine on July 29 left just 316 survivors from a ship's crew of 1200, making it "the worst American catastrophe at sea during the entire war."[21] It served as a painful reminder of the Japanese capability and determination to defend their homeland. Truman's attention occasionally gravitated to the prospects for the atomic bomb, and its likely consequences for the war against Japan. Yet, he had no need to constantly monitor the situation. Obviously aware that the bomb would soon be deployed, the president spoke with the small contingent of White House press corps members on board the *Augusta* on August 3, and he gave them a scoop they were unable to use before the ship reached port. He told them that the United States had developed a new and powerful weapon that might hasten the end of the war.

In the northwest Atlantic on Sunday evening, August 5, at the actual time the bomb exploded over Hiroshima, Truman may well have been watching the comedy/mystery film "Thin Man Goes Home" starring William Powell and Myrna Loy. Not until the next day as he ate his lunch in the sailors' mess did he receive the first reports about the mission Tibbets and his crew completed. Stimson informed him that the "big bomb" had been used on Hiroshima and that "first reports indicate complete success which was even more conspicuous than earlier test." According to his own later account, Truman "was deeply moved." He passed along the news to Byrnes and then with gushing enthusiasm proclaimed to the sailors gathered with him that "this is the greatest thing in history. It is time for us to get home." A further message arrived that confirmed the initial assessment. With palpable excitement Truman informed his mess hall compatriots of the powerful new bomb, which he described "as twenty thousand times as powerful as a ton of TNT." Then he raced to the ship's wardroom to share the news with the *Augusta*'s officers. An observant journalist remembers him almost running as he moved about the ship "spreading the news." As the president later put it,

---

[21] For a powerful description of the sinking of the *Indianapolis* and the harrowing ordeal of its survivors see Stanley Weintraub, *The Last Great Victory*, pp. 295–298, 307–310, 326–328, 345–347, 366–371; direct quotation from p. 369.

he could not keep back his "expectation that the Pacific war might now be brought to a speedy end."[22] Here lay his primary and deepest hope regarding the impact of the atomic bomb.

The real audience for Truman's thoughts on the bomb did not reside on board the USS *Augusta*, however, but in Japan. Provision had been made for a statement, prepared before he left for Potsdam, to be issued under the president's name as soon as confirmation came through on the success of the first atomic bombing mission. As his ship ploughed its way back to Newport News, this statement was distributed far and wide. It gave basic details of the attack against Hiroshima, and an elemental description both of the power of the new weapon and the scientific effort that allowed the Anglo-Americans to win "the battle of the laboratories" against the Germans to produce it successfully. He described the atomic bomb as harnessing "the basic power of the universe." In words that might have been expected to penetrate through to the purported descendant of the Sun God then sitting on the Japanese throne, the American leader held that "the force from which the sun draws its power has been loosed against those who brought war to the Far East." Clearly intent on shocking and intimidating the Japanese, Truman warned that the United States was "now prepared to obliterate more rapidly and completely every productive enterprise" that lay above ground in any city in Japan. There should be no mistake, he threatened, "we shall completely destroy Japan's power to make war." Piling on the verbal pressure he explained that the Potsdam ultimatum had been issued "to spare the Japanese people from utter destruction," but that Japanese leaders had rejected it. This time they should act differently. In words that implied the use of further atomic bombs he uttered a brutal warning to the Japanese leadership: "If they do not now accept our terms they may expect a rain of ruin from the air, the likes of which has never been seen on this earth." Notably, he further advised that "behind this air attack will follow sea and land forces in such numbers and power as they have not yet seen and with the fighting skill of which they are already well aware."[23] Naturally, Truman hoped that the awesome display of airpower over Hiroshima would obviate the need to utilize the sea and land forces.

[22] For Truman's account, which includes the two messages he received, see *Year of Decisions*, pp. 464–465. Also see Weintraub, *The Last Great Victory*, pp. 420–421, which includes the observation of the journalist Merriman Smith.

[23] See Statement by the President Announcing the Use of the A-bomb at Hiroshima, August 6, 1945, *Public Papers of the Presidents: Harry S. Truman 1945* (Washington, D.C., 1961), pp. 197–200.

On board the *Augusta* Truman and Byrnes drew satisfaction from the successful use of the atomic bomb. Indicative of his domestic political focus Byrnes recalled how as director of war mobilization he had become "worried about the huge expenditure and feared repercussions because he had doubt of its working." Stimson, however, had reassured him. Truman suppressed any comment on his own wartime dealings with Stimson and generously spoke to the importance of having men like the secretary of war "who have the respect of people" and whom Congress held in such regard to authorize such "huge expenditures in secrecy."[24] Now, the two politicians hoped, the huge amounts expended on the Manhattan Project would pay such notable political dividends in forcing Japan's defeat so as to disarm even the most severe fiscal critics. The use of the bomb hopefully would validate the enormous scientific and financial endeavor pursued under Roosevelt's administration.

Neither Truman nor Byrnes raised any concerns regarding whether the atomic bomb was a legitimate weapon of war. Nor did either man raise any questions about the plans to use further bombs against the Japanese. Truman continued to act as a sort of "chairman of the board" who validated and confirmed recommendations that came up to him from subordinates.[25] He had stepped into FDR's shoes and also into his assumptions that the weapon should be used to secure victory in the war. Furthermore, his approval of the use of the atomic bomb reflected the Rooseveltian preference to "achieve complete victory at the lowest cost in American lives." The atomic bomb proved yet another arrow in the impressive quiver of America's "industrial might and technological prowess," which allowed U.S. casualties to be kept so light relative to the losses of other major participants in the war. Samuel Walker correctly noted that "Truman inherited from Roosevelt the strategy of keeping American losses to a minimum, and he was committed to carrying it out for the remainder of the war."[26]

Eager to force Japan's defeat before paying any invasion's high cost in American blood, Truman allowed the predetermined policy to proceed. While numerous concerned commentators writing from a post-Hiroshima perspective have sought to supply all kinds of alternatives to the atomic bomb for the American president's use, he operated in a pre-Hiroshima

---

[24] Entry August 6, 1945, Walter Brown's Diary, Byrnes Papers, Folder 602.
[25] Alonzo Hamby refers to Truman as "chairman of the board" in *Man of the People*, p. 324.
[26] See J. Samuel Walker, *Prompt and Utter Destruction: Truman and the Use of Atomic Bombs against Japan* (Chapel Hill, NC, 1997), p. 9.

PHOTO 10. Fat Man, the atomic bomb detonated over Nagasaki. (Courtesy Harry S. Truman Presidential Library.)

world. Truman and his associates like Byrnes didn't seek to avoid using the bomb, and those who focus on "alternatives" distort history by overemphasizing them.[27] As Barton Bernstein persuasively clarified, the American leaders "easily rejected or never considered most of the so-called alternatives to the bomb."[28] They saw no reason to do so because they viewed the atomic bomb as another weapon in the Allied arsenal along with such complements – *not* alternatives – as the naval blockade, continued conventional bombing, the threat of invasion, and Soviet entry into the war. Together, they hoped, these might secure a Japanese surrender before American troops waded ashore on the southern plains of Kyushu.

Forcing a Japanese surrender formed the prism through which Truman also viewed both the use of a second atomic bomb and the Soviet Union's decision to enter the war. By the time the president arrived safely back on

---

[27] The most recent work to focus attention on "alternatives" is Tsuyoshi Hasegawa's *Racing the Enemy: Stalin, Truman, and the Surrender of Japan* (Cambridge, MA, 2005), see especially pp. 295–299.

[28] Bernstein, "Understanding the Atomic Bomb and the Japanese Surrender," p. 235.

American soil on August 7 preparations had begun to ready the other available atomic bomb, known as "Fat Man," for use in accord with established plans. Neither further decisions nor orders were needed. The governing strategy called for the dropping of a second bomb a few days after the first to convey to Japanese decision makers that the United States had an unlimited supply of them and to drive home unmistakably the warnings about the "rain of ruin from the air." The initial plan had been to use the second weapon on August 11 but fears of bad weather forced the crews on Tinian to move the date forward to August 9. This didn't upset the ordnance experts readying "Fat Man" because, as one of them recalled, "everyone felt that the sooner we could get off another mission, the more likely it was that the Japanese would feel that we had large quantities of the devices and would surrender sooner."[29] Coincident with these preparations the United States continued its massive conventional bombing efforts, and also dropped leaflets over Japanese cities informing their residents of Hiroshima's destruction and calling upon them to evacuate their cities immediately.

While the Americans readied their next atomic assault, the Soviet Union pounded another nail in the coffin of Japan's war effort on August 8 when they declared war and soon thereafter launched a powerful attack on Japanese forces in Manchuria. The Soviets certainly had some sense of the force of the new weapon and recognized, it would seem, that they must enter the war immediately in case the Hiroshima bombing quickly persuaded the Japanese to surrender.[30] They conveniently put aside their supposed need to reach a satisfactory settlement with the Chinese regarding postwar arrangements in north Asia in order to establish themselves formally as opponents of Japan. Late in the afternoon of August 8 Molotov called in Japanese Ambassador Sato and broke the news to him, thereby ending whatever remaining hopes existed in Tokyo that the Soviets might serve as an intermediary for peace negotiations. Later in the evening Stalin met with U.S. Ambassador Harriman and his embassy counselor, George Kennan. Harriman appropriately voiced the official American position and expressed "his gratification at the fact that we were once again allies."[31] They thereupon discussed initial reports of

[29] Ensign Bernard J. O'Keefe, a member of the assembly team, quoted in Weintraub, *The Last Great Victory*, p. 446.
[30] On Soviet reactions to the Hiroshima bombing and for the Soviet decision to declare war on Japan see David Holloway's *Stalin and the Bomb*, pp. 127–129; and Hasegawa, *Racing the Enemy*, pp. 186–191.
[31] Memorandum of conversation, August 8, 1945, Harriman Papers, Box 181.

Soviet military actions and the likely impact of the atomic bomb on the Japanese.

The Americans appreciated well that the Soviets had rushed their declaration of war, but the reigning American assumption, as Byrnes had learned at Potsdam, held that the Soviets would have their way in Manchuria regardless of whatever happened elsewhere in the Pacific theater. Truman took the Soviet intervention in stride and with real satisfaction. He made a brief announcement to White House reporters that "Russia has declared war on Japan," but nonetheless he deemed the matter as "so important" he did it in person with Secretary Byrnes and Admiral Leahy flanking him. Presumably he wanted to add to the pressure on the Japanese without engaging in any effusive commentary that might exaggerate the extent of the Soviet contribution to Japan's ultimate defeat. In his radio report on the Potsdam Conference given during the evening of August 9, Truman referred to Soviet entry into the war in the Pacific and "gladly welcomed into this struggle against the last of the Axis aggressors our gallant and victorious ally against the Nazis."[32] Privately, Truman affirmed to his aides that he had gone to Potsdam "entirely for the purpose of making sure that Stalin would come in then [August 15] or earlier if possible."[33] He expressed no regret whatsoever at his efforts. The contentions by the historian Tsuyoshi Hasegawa that Truman felt a "sense of betrayal" at the Soviet entry into the war and that Truman was a "disappointed man" because of the Soviet action are not substantiated by the historical evidence.[34]

Truman's radio address contained further pointed warnings to the Japanese. Truman declared to the American people and beyond them to an audience that he hoped included Japan's leadership that "the first atomic bomb was dropped on Hiroshima, a military base. That was because we wished," he continued, "in this first attack to avoid in so far as possible, the killing of civilians." Then he cautioned that the first attack must be understood as "only a warning of things to come." Raising the stakes still further in the psychological warfare effort to intimidate the enemy, Truman apprised all his listeners that "if Japan does not surrender, bombs will have to be dropped on war industries and, unfortunately, thousands of civilian lives will be lost." He urged "Japanese civilians to

---

[32] Radio Report of the President to the Nation, August 9, 1945, *Department of State Bulletin*, Vol. 13 (August 12, 1945), p. 209.

[33] See Ayers's diary entry, August 9, 1945, in Robert H. Ferrell, ed., *Truman in the White House: The Diary of Eben A. Ayers* (Columbia, MO, 1991), p. 62.

[34] See Hasegawa, *Racing the Enemy*, pp. 193–194.

leave industrial cities immediately, and save themselves from destruction."[35] Unfortunately for the residents of the Japanese city of Nagasaki before any of them could learn in translation of Truman's latest warning their city had been subjected to the second atomic attack.

The primary target for the crew of *Bock's Car*, which delivered the "Fat Man" bomb, was the Kyushu city of Kokura, but cloud, smoke, and smog obscured that target. Instead, the Americans flew on to the secondary target, the important port of Nagasaki in western Kyushu, home to Mitsubishi shipyards and industrial plants.[36] There the plane commanded

PHOTO II. View of the Mitsubishi Torpedo Plant in Nagasaki, following the atomic bomb explosion, August 1945. (Courtesy Harry S. Truman Presidential Library.)

[35] Radio Report of the President to the Nation, August 9, 1945, *Department of State Bulletin*, Vol. 13 (August 12, 1945), p. 212.
[36] On the bombing of Nagasaki see Weintraub, *The Last Great Victory*, pp. 481–491. Tsuyoshi Hasegawa rather strangely asks in his *Racing the Enemy*, p. 194, "why, given the knowledge that the Soviets had entered the war, didn't Truman order the suspension or postponement of the Nagasaki bomb?" This question reveals a complete lack of understanding of the American strategy to "shock" the Japanese into surrender.

by Maj. Charles Sweeney dropped the second atomic bomb without warning on the city soon after 11:00 A.M. The bomb exploded right over the Immaculate Conception Catholic Cathedral located in the Urakami district of the city. Its effect was devastating, but not comparable to that inflicted on Hiroshima. Casualty estimates for immediate deaths reached approximately 45,000 with a similar number injured, of whom many died, over the ensuing weeks and months. More than a third of Nagasaki was destroyed, but the center of the city was spared because the steep hills that surrounded it served to mitigate the bomb's impact.

Although the initial Japanese reports downplayed the damage, word reached Tokyo of the use of a second atomic bomb. Yet again a solitary plane delivered a horrific blow that far exceeded what could have been inflicted by hundreds of B-29s armed with conventional bombs. The planned message to the Japanese reverberated one more time – surrender or face utter destruction. Mercifully, the message began to be heard in Tokyo.

CHAPTER 6

The Japanese Surrender

The first of the two nuclear weapons used in war caused a blinding explosion over the center of Hiroshima. It produced enormous damage and killed approximately eighty thousand people while wounding a similar number. Many of the maimed died soon thereafter from the effects of their exposure to the radioactivity let loose by the explosion. The bomb caused carnage and devastation for five square miles. One observer who entered Hiroshima on August 7 described it simply as "a city completely destroyed." He recalled it as an "indescribable spectacle," indeed as "a macabre vision which staggered the imagination."[1] Scenes of horror and suffering overwhelmed those who sought to rescue the victims of the unprecedented assault.

Hiroshima contained military targets – a military headquarters, an assembly area for troops, a communications center, and a port that served as the main embarkation center for China – yet its civilian residents suffered greatly from the destructive power of the atomic blast. The Japanese government emphasized the civilian nature of the target in the protest it transmitted to the United States through the good offices of the Swiss government on August 9. The statement contested Truman's claim that Hiroshima counted as a military target noting that the city lacked "military fortifications or installations." It zeroed in on the indiscriminate nature of the bomb, pointing out that "the zone of damage spread over a wide area and all persons within this area, without discrimination as to belligerents and non-belligerents and irrespective of sex or

---

[1] The observer was a Spanish Jesuit priest, Pedro Arrupe. See his recollections in "Surviving the Atomic Bomb," in Pedro Arrupe, *Essential Writings* (Maryknoll, NY, 2004), pp. 40–45.

PHOTO 12. Hiroshima in ruins, August 1945. (Courtesy Harry S. Truman Presidential Library.)

age, were killed or wounded by the blast and radiated heat." It presented the enormous and indiscriminate slaughter as contrary to the "basic principles of the international rules of warfare which state that a belligerent does not enjoy an unrestricted right in the choice of methods of attack and that the belligerent shall not make use of any weapon which would cause unnecessary suffering."[2]

Initial reports of the extensive damage to Hiroshima reached Tokyo beginning on August 7. A cabinet meeting on that day reviewed the partial and somewhat confusing information and the associated details of Truman's threatening statement calling for immediate surrender. The knowledge that more bombs might be on their way was well understood as of August 8 by certain key civilian officials, although the Japanese military remained committed to their *Ketsu-Go* strategy whatever the awful damage to Hiroshima. As such, the Japanese authorities formally

---

[2] The cable from Tokyo (Togo) to Bern, August 9, 1945 including the text of the protest is included in the materials gathered in Byrnes Papers, Folder 571.

held back from any decision in reaction to the American threat. But Foreign Minister Togo, the leading civilian proponent of "peace" within the government, planted the seeds for an eventual change in policy when he visited the Imperial Palace on August 8 and briefed Emperor Hirohito. As the historian Tristan Grunow explained, Togo "used the bombing of Hiroshima and American broadcasts promising to drop more bombs on Japan to press his argument for ending the war, urging that Japan could 'seize the opportunity' to surrender quickly."[3] Togo recalled that the emperor agreed, and in fact observed that "now that such a new weapon has appeared, it has become less and less possible to continue war. ... So my wish is to make such arrangements as will end the war as soon as possible."[4] The emperor's decision, it should be noted, came before any news of a Soviet declaration of war reached him, and it confirms the decisive importance of the atomic attack on Hiroshima in forcing the ultimate Japanese surrender. It proved, however, a difficult task to translate this imperial wish, which did not specify any detailed terms of surrender, into a formal policy decision because the Japanese military proved quite resistant to any notion of surrender.

The Supreme War Leadership Council met on August 9 to review the proper course for Japan. By this time its members also had before them the damaging news of the Soviet declaration of war to consider. This body [the Big Six] brought together both the key civilian and military leadership of Japan and its members divided into war and peace factions. According to one participant "a rather bullish atmosphere" prevailed at the outset of their morning meeting.[5] After some hours of debate and discussion Prime Minister Suzuki, Foreign Minister Shigenori Togo, and, rather hesitantly, Navy Minister Mitsumasa Yonai favored the acceptance of the Potsdam terms with the important and essential exception of preserving the *kokutai* – the Japanese imperial system guaranteeing the sacred position and prerogatives of the emperor. But War Minister Korechika Anami and the army and navy chiefs, General Yoshijiro Umezu and Admiral Soemu Toyoda, would not agree to such terms. They preferred to fight a decisive homeland battle regardless of the cost in Japanese lives unless the allies agreed to the additional conditions of "self-disarmament, Japanese control of any war-crimes trials, and, above all, no Allied

---

[3] Tristan Grunow, "A Reexamination of the 'Shock of Hiroshima': The Japanese Bomb Projects and the Surrender Decision," *The Journal of American-East Asian Relations*, Vol. 12, Nos. 3–4 (Fall-Winter, 2008), p. 175.

[4] Quoted in Grunow, p. 175.

[5] Admiral Toyoda quoted from his memoirs in Frank, *Downfall*, p. 291.

occupation of Japan." Richard B. Frank has tellingly clarified that "these terms would permit, at some later and better moment, Japan's warriors to inculcate a myth that they were never really defeated and only of their own volition laid down arms to spare the world more ravages of war."[6]

Into the midst of their meeting came the initial news of the atomic bombing of Nagasaki.[7] This report shattered any doubts concerning the American capability to use more than one weapon. Prime Minister Suzuki now began to fear that "the United States, instead of staging the invasion of Japan, will keep on dropping atomic bombs."[8] But the second bomb did not alter the firmly held positions of the Japanese leaders. No consensus emerged to support the acceptance of the Potsdam terms with the proviso regarding the preservation of the imperial system. Indeed, as Frank has shown, it seems likely that Suzuki came to the Imperial Palace early in the afternoon of August 9 and recommended acceptance of the Potsdam terms with the *four* conditions that represented "the lowest common denominator of agreement within the Big Six."[9] These conditions most certainly would have been interpreted by the Truman administration as a clear rejection of the Potsdam terms. Only some intense lobbying by the indefatigable senior statesman Prince Fuminaro Konoe of the emperor's brother Prince Takamatsu and also by former foreign minister Mamoru Sigemitsu of the emperor's key aide Koichi Kido raised questions in the Imperial Palace about this course.[10]

Meanwhile, Suzuki chaired a meeting of his full cabinet during the afternoon of August 9. Again, no consensus emerged despite hours of discussion. As the Japanese procedures called for unanimity for any decision to be presented to the emperor, Suzuki left for the palace to explain the situation. Technically he should have resigned and advised the emperor to appoint another prime minister to form a government, but he did not. Instead he advised Hirohito to convene an imperial conference to allow the emperor to hear the arguments of the members of the Supreme War Leadership Council.[11] And so it was that the Big Six along with Baron

---

[6] Frank, *Downfall*, p. 291. My summary of the August 9 meeting and the outline of the additional conditions of the Japanese military also are drawn from Frank, pp. 290–291.

[7] On the impact of the second atomic bomb see Sadao Asada, "The Shock of the Atomic Bomb and Japan's Decision to Surrender – A Reconsideration," *Pacific Historical Review*, Vol. 67 (November, 1998), pp. 490–493.

[8] Suzuki quoted in Asada, "The Shock of the Atomic Bomb," p. 491.

[9] Frank, *Downfall*, p. 291.

[10] Frank, *Downfall*, p. 291. Also see Hasegawa, *Racing the Enemy*, pp. 205–209.

[11] Sadao Asada argues that Suzuki made his suggestion based on a previous understanding with Emperor Hirohito. See Asada, "The Shock of the Atomic Bomb and Japan's Decision to Surrender," p. 495.

Kiichiro Hiranuma, the president of the Privy Council, and a few aides gathered in an underground air-raid shelter a few minutes before midnight on August 9 and bowed low as the emperor entered the room. According to the most measured accounts of this meeting Suzuki again presented the *four* condition terms as the consensus view of the Council.[12] Foreign Minister Togo made the case for surrender with only the insistence on preserving the emperor's prerogatives. Anami, Umezu, and Toyoda still vigorously opposed this position. Anami spoke of resolutely proceeding with the prosecution of the war and declared that "if the people of Japan went into the decisive battle in the homeland determined to display the full measure of patriotism and to fight to the very last, Japan would be able to avert the crisis facing her."[13] Hiranuma and Suzuki lent some indirect support to Togo's position and spoke of the developing unrest within the Japanese population and the prospect of its increasing as bombing continued.

Eventually, Suzuki asked the emperor to decide between the two proposals. This he did. He concluded that "the time has come when we must bear the unbearable." Claiming that he could not bear to see his people suffer any longer, Hirohito held that world peace must be restored and his nation relieved from its terrible distress. Associating himself with his ancestor, the Emperor Meiji, at the time Japan had been forced to back down from some of its demands on China at the conclusion of the Sino-Japanese War in 1894–1895, Hirohito concluded: "I swallow my own tears and give my sanction to the proposal to accept the Allied proclamation on the basis outlined by the Foreign Minister."[14] His verdict given, he then left the room. The reasons for his decision have been much debated by historians but there is little reason to question the genuineness of Hirohito's desire to bring the suffering of his people to an end. The emperor who had enthusiastically supported the Japanese predatory expansion in China in the nineteen thirties, and who had appointed General Tojo Hideki as prime minister in October 1941 and supported the reckless policies that led to the Pacific War now realized the failure of the Japanese imperialist venture. He had come to understand clearly, and in a way that his military leaders refused to comprehend, that the defense of the homeland was hopeless. Assuredly, the atomic bombings of

---

[12] See Frank, *Downfall*, pp. 293–296; and the classic account provided in Robert J. C. Butow, *Japan's Decision to Surrender* (Stanford, 1954), pp. 168–176.

[13] For Anami's position see Butow, *Japan's Decision to Surrender*, p. 170.

[14] See Hirohito's full statement in Butow, *Japan's Decision to Surrender*, pp. 175–176.

Hiroshima and Nagasaki when combined with the Soviet declaration of war brought matters to a head for him, and brought him decisively to the side of the cabinet faction that wanted to negotiate a peace. In his own crucial deliberations the atomic attacks appeared to weigh most heavily.[15] So the serious work of negotiation began protected by the emperor's imprimatur.

Prime Minister Suzuki asked the gathered officials to accept the emperor's decision, and then promptly gathered together the members of his full cabinet. "Sometime between 3:00 and 4:00 A.M.," as Richard Frank recounts, "the ministers officially adopted the 'Imperial decision,' therefore swaddling the Emperor's words spoken only an hour before in legal force."[16] Notably at this meeting Anami clarified with Suzuki that Japan would fight on if the Allies refused to accede to the Japanese demand regarding the emperor's authority. With this decision made, foreign ministry officials quickly dispatched cables through their official intermediaries in Berne advising the Allies that Japan would accept the Potsdam terms with the crucial proviso that this would "not comprise any demand which prejudices the prerogatives of His Majesty as a Sovereign Ruler." In reality the Japanese response represented a severe qualification of the Potsdam unconditional surrender terms for it sought to preserve the supremacy of the emperor within Japan with all that implied. The Japanese note expressed the sincere hope that "this understanding is warranted" and requested that "an explicit indication to that effect will be speedily forthcoming."[17]

The Japanese had made their decision and now it fell to the United States and its allies to consider Japan's offer. Rather surprisingly the key American officials were not gathered together in fervent expectation of an immediate Japanese surrender. Indeed, there had been little planning for such an eventuality. As Richard Frank ably has demonstrated, there had been no decision on Truman's part to take any measures to begin the shift from a wartime to a peacetime economy. Clearly, the president assumed no

---

[15] On the significance of the atomic bomb in forcing the decision of the Japanese see the helpful discussion in Robert P. Newman, *Truman and the Hiroshima Cult* (East Lansing, MI, 1995), pp. 101–103.

[16] Frank, *Downfall*, p. 296.

[17] The Japanese note is included in Swiss Charge d'Affaires Grassli to Secretary Byrnes, August 10, 1945, printed in *Department of State Bulletin*, Vol. 13 (August 12, 1945), p. 205. Through their officials in Berne and Stockholm the Japanese also communicated their willingness to surrender to the governments of Great Britain, China, and the Soviet Union.

sudden Japanese concession. Secretary of War Stimson even planned to depart Washington on August 10 for some days of vacation, "an eloquent indicator of how far official Washington believed that Japan remained from surrender even after two atomic bombs."[18] Truman had not spent any inordinate amount of time following his return to the White House late on August 7 fixated on the atomic bomb. Stimson had briefed him on the huge damage done to Hiroshima and the numerous casualties, and the president evidently began to feel some reservations about the destruction. On August 9 Truman replied to a letter from Georgia Senator Richard Russell that called for the continued atomic bombing of Japan by explaining that "I know that Japan is a terribly cruel and uncivilized nation in warfare but I can't bring myself to believe that, because they are beasts, we should act in the same manner." He continued that "for myself, I certainly regret the necessity of wiping out whole populations because of the 'pigheadedness' of the leaders of a nation and, for your information, I am not going to do it until it is absolutely necessary.... My object is to save as many American lives as possible but I also have a humane feeling for the women and children in Japan."[19] Whatever Truman's developing qualms about the use of the atomic bombs, there had been no extensive discussion of how the United States might respond to a Japanese surrender containing the proviso regarding the emperor. Once again policy would be formulated quickly.

The first news of the Japanese offer came courtesy of the MAGIC code breakers and then from Army radio monitors who gathered reports from Radio Tokyo. By early morning (Washington time) Truman determined that these reports, while not official, warranted discussion and he asked Admiral Leahy to gather Stimson, Byrnes, and Forrestal together at 9:00 A.M. to review the situation. At this meeting Leahy and Stimson encouraged Truman to accept the Japanese offer, which they incorrectly interpreted as meaning the retention of Hirohito in some very limited ceremonial role. Byrnes, motivated by his domestic political concerns, held back and argued that the United States could not accept Japan's conditions for surrender.[20] According to what he later told his associate Walter Brown, the secretary of state pointed to the "unconditional surrender" demands of the Potsdam Declaration and then expressed his concern at why "we should go further

---

[18] Frank, *Downfall*, p. 300.
[19] Truman to Russell, August 9, 1945, Official File, Truman Papers.
[20] Robertson emphasizes "domestic politics" as Byrnes's "primary motivation" in *Sly and Able*, p. 435–436.

[in concessions] than we were willing to go at Potsdam when we had no atomic bomb, and Russia was not in the war." Byrnes's intervention proved successful, and thus the White House meeting shelved Leahy's proposed memorandum simply accepting the Japanese offer – a position which, Byrnes remarked later that day, "would have led to [the] crucifixion of [the] President."[21] Instead Truman accepted the suggestion of Navy Secretary Forrestal that "we might in our reply indicate willingness to accept, yet define the terms of surrender in such a manner that the intents and purposes of the Potsdam Declaration would be clearly accomplished."[22] The president charged Byrnes with drafting such a reply, which he did with superb skill aided by his counselor, Benjamin Cohen, and the State Department's Japanese experts led by Joseph Grew.

Byrnes returned to the White House by noon with his masterful draft reply, and he and Truman discussed it over lunch and prepared for a full meeting of the cabinet at 2:00 P.M. They also drafted messages to London, Moscow, and Chungking requesting the approval of the terms that set forth that "from the moment of surrender the authority of the Emperor and the Japanese Government to rule the state shall be subject to the Supreme Commander of the Allied powers who will take such steps as he deems proper to effectuate the surrender terms." The terms placed the burden on the emperor to call on all Japanese forces to cease their operations and to surrender their arms and made specific provisions for prisoners of war. Then, in unmistakable terms, the proposed response made clear that "the ultimate form of government of Japan shall, in accordance with the Potsdam Declaration, be established by the freely expressed will of the Japanese people." It promised that "the armed forces of the Allied Powers will remain in Japan until the purposes set forth in the Potsdam Declaration are achieved."[23] This hardly constituted any "explicit guarantee that the Imperial institution would continue, much less that Hirohito would remain on the throne."[24] No long-term guarantees were extended to Hirohito and, indeed, in an August 10 conversation with a Democratic

---

[21] Diary entry, August 10, 1945, Brown Diary, Byrnes Papers, Folder 602. Byrnes was angry at Leahy's actions and told Brown that "Leahy still thought he was Secretary of State, just as he was under Roosevelt, and he had to show him differently."

[22] Truman, *Year of Decisions*, p. 472.

[23] For the early draft of Byrnes's proposed response see Truman, *Year of Decisions*, p. 473. The slightly modified final version that went to the Japanese is included in Byrnes to Swiss Charge d'Affaires Grassli, August 11, 1945, *Department of State Bulletin*, Vol. 13 (August 12, 1945), pp. 205–206.

[24] Frank, *Downfall*, p. 302.

senator confidante, Truman branded the emperor as "a war criminal just as much as Hitler or Mussolini, in many respects, [who] was now trying to weasel his nation out of war, [while] preserving its essentially totalitarian structure."[25] Nonetheless, the seasoned politician pragmatically recognized the advantage in retaining the emperor at least to use him to help secure the surrender of the enormous Japanese forces still in the field.

Eager to end the war without any further American losses, the Truman administration asked their allies for a speedy response to the terms that Byrnes drafted. The British and the Chinese soon advised of their essential agreement. Soviet approval came more grudgingly as Ambassador Harriman discovered when he met with Molotov late in the evening of August 10. The Soviet foreign minister initially tried to delay his nation's response. When Harriman insisted on an answer, Molotov met with him and the British ambassador at 2:00 A.M. to provide it. He indicated agreement with the response to the Japanese but, in the case of an affirmative reply, he asserted that "the Allied Powers should reach an agreement on the candidacy or candidacies for representation of the Allied High Command to which the Japanese Emperor and the Japanese Government are to be subordinated."

Harriman followed up and discerned that the Soviets expected to play a major role in the occupation, something incidentally that Stalin had discussed at length with his military and political advisers in the preceding months.[26] Molotov even speculated that "it was conceivable that there might be two Supreme Commanders; [Soviet General] Vasilevski and [General] MacArthur." With barely controlled anger Harriman branded such an arrangement as "absolutely inadmissible." Molotov told the ambassador bluntly that regardless of his personal thoughts the Soviets wanted the message transmitted to Washington. Harriman agreed to do so, but with a parting flourish drew to Molotov's attention "that the United States had carried the main burden of the war in the Pacific on its shoulders for four years. It had therefore kept the Japanese off the Soviet's back. The Soviet government had been at war for two days. It was only just that the Soviet government should place in American hands the choice as to who would be Supreme Commander. The present Soviet position was absolutely impossible." Molotov apparently reported back to Stalin on

---

[25] This was the report of a *Time* journalist who subsequently interviewed Truman's inter-locutor as quoted in Barton J. Bernstein, "Commentary" on Tsuyoshi Hasegawa, *Racing the Enemy* in H-Diplo Roundtable, text p. 28.

[26] See Vladislav M. Zubok, *A Failed Empire: The Soviet Union in the Cold War from Stalin to Gorbachev* (Chapel Hill, NC, 2007), pp. 26–27.

Harriman's strongly negative reaction against their provocative gambit to muscle in on the occupation. By the time Harriman returned to his embassy office Stalin's translator Vladimir Pavlov called to retreat somewhat. He clarified that the Soviets sought only "consultation" rather than "agreement" on the occupation arrangements.[27] Harriman quickly conveyed the Soviet response back to Washington.

Once the approvals from the Allies arrived Byrnes issued the response on behalf of all four governments and placed the onus for a decision back on the policy makers in Tokyo, especially Hirohito. Truman's support for Byrnes's astute tactical move now forced the Japanese leaders to face squarely the reality that they truly must admit defeat and subject themselves to a full occupation. While Truman and the Allied governments waited hopefully for a positive Japanese response to this clear demand, American military leaders made no assumptions of a quick Japanese capitulation. As Michael Gordin has clarified so well, they did not assume that two atomic bombs would secure the necessary Japanese surrender. On August 10, the very day that Byrnes dispatched his message, Gen. Carl Spaatz, Commander of the U.S. Strategic Air Forces in the Pacific, cabled from his Guam headquarters back to Gen. Lauris Norstad in the Plans Division of the Army Air Force in the Pentagon that he strongly recommended "that the next Centerboard [i.e., atomic strike] be Tokio [sic]." As he saw it, "more destruction probably would be obtained from choosing a clean target but it is believed that the psychological effect on the government officials still remaining in Tokio is more important at this time than destruction."[28] General Groves eagerly assured his superiors that further bombs would be deliverable as of late August. Thankfully, Truman was never forced to order the use of a third weapon because of the decisions made in Tokyo.

The Allies demanded that the emperor subject himself to the authority of an American general and, in the end, he agreed to this course. Again, however, only after a major division occurred among his advisers.[29] While Foreign Minister Togo recommended immediate acceptance of the Allied

[27] The account of this meeting and the various texts involved are included in Memorandum of Conversation, August 10, 1945, W. Averell Harriman Papers, Manuscripts Division, Library of Congress, Box 181.

[28] Spaatz quoted in Gordin, *Five Days in August*, p. 98. Gordin further clarifies the military's thinking about the use of additional weapons in his *Five Days in August*, pp. 98–101.

[29] The story of the divisions in Japan over the surrender terms is told with dramatic flair in William Craig, *The Fall of Japan* (New York, 1967), pp. 135–201. Also see Richard Frank's incisive account in *Downfall*, pp. 308–321.

terms, War Minister Anami now backed by Baron Hiranuma opposed them fearing the fate of the emperor and his sacred role. Inside the War Ministry, and among army and navy officers in the field, suggestions that Japan should surrender met with disbelief and rejection. Illustrative were the combative yet deluded views of General Yasuji Okamura, the commander of Japanese armies in China, who held that "the humiliating peace terms which have been reported by foreign broadcasts are tantamount to liquidating the Japanese empire which is now shining in all its glory and no subject of the empire can on any account submit to them." He maintained that Japan should "fight to the end, determined that the whole army should die an honorable death without being distracted by the enemy's peace offensive."[30] In an increasingly tumultuous situation in the Japanese capital, agitated military officers geared up to challenge and reverse any decision to accept the Potsdam terms.

Tracing in detail the intrigues and internecine battles among Japanese civilian and military figures is beyond the scope of this study, but it must be said that the harrowing ordeal of the peace faction gives the lie to any notion of a Japan just waiting to surrender. Fortunately Hirohito, supported by his chief aide Kido, decided to accept the terms of the Byrnes note as the best he could expect for himself and his dynasty.[31] He thereupon secured the firm endorsement of the princes of the imperial family at a meeting on August 12 and these royal relatives eventually played a helpful role in implementing his decision. Yet his War Cabinet remained divided, and on August 14 the emperor had to again intervene directly in a meeting of the Supreme War Council along with other officials. He listened to Anami, Toyoda, and Umezu repeat their arguments of August 9 but rejected them firmly. "I have surveyed the conditions prevailing in Japan and in the world," he told his officials, "and it is my belief that a continuation of the war promises nothing but additional destruction." He insisted that Japan must accept the Allied terms. Furthermore, he agreed to make a broadcast to his people explaining the necessity of ending the war.[32] The emperor and his officials shed tears of sorrow as he finally called upon each man present "to exert himself to the utmost so that we

---

[30] Okamura quoted in Ronald H. Spector, *In the Ruins of Empire: The Japanese Surrender and the Battle for Postwar Asia* (New York, 2007), p. 23; and Hastings, *Retribution*, p. 509.

[31] Hasegawa, *Racing the Enemy*, pp. 230–233.

[32] On the August 14 meeting see Frank, *Downfall*, pp. 314–315; and Butow, *Japan's Decision to Surrender*, pp. 206–209.

may meet the trying days which lie ahead."[33] The decision made, the aged and exhausted Suzuki convened the cabinet, which then ratified the emperor's wishes. Thereupon the foreign ministry transmitted this news to the four Allied powers through their intermediaries in Berne and Stockholm.

One might think that action should have ended matters, but hardly so. Gerhard Weinberg has summarized well that "military figures in key positions in the capital tried to kill their opponents, seize and destroy the recording with the Emperor's broadcast to the people of Japan, and take over power with the intention of continuing the war."[34] On the evening of August 14 fanatical young officers unsuccessfully targeted Prime Minister Suzuki, Baron Hiranuma, and the emperor's chief aide Marquis Kido. Rebellious troops occupied the Imperial Palace grounds and killed General Takeshi Mori of the Imperial Guards Division in the process.[35] Happily for Japan and for peace, Anami and Umezu refused to endorse plans for a full-blown coup and officers loyal to the emperor put down the rebellion. Anami and a number of military officials painfully salved the bitter disgrace of surrender by committing ritual suicide. Still, Suzuki's government stayed in place and readied itself for the burdens of surrender, and only then submitted its resignation. Nonetheless, it was, as Weinberg concluded in his characteristically balanced fashion, "a close call, and in a way shows that the earlier fears of the peace advocates within the government, that any open move to end the war could lead to a coup which would prolong rather than shorten the conflict, was warranted."[36]

On August 15 the Japanese citizenry heard Hirohito's prerecorded speech played over the radio in which he announced that he had accepted the terms set forth by the Allies. The war must end, said the man who sat "by the Grace of Heaven" upon "the Throne occupied by the same Dynasty changeless through ages eternal." As Robert Butow pointed out the emperor never mentioned such words as "defeat," "surrender," and "capitulation," but framed the need for Japan's concession in terms of Japanese interests. Hirohito explained to his people that "the war situation has developed not necessarily to Japan's advantage, while the general trends of the world have all turned against her interest." He also specifically mentioned that "the enemy has begun to develop a new and most cruel bomb, the power of which to do damage is indeed incalculable,

---

[33] Hirohito's words are recorded in Butow, *Japan's Decision to Surrender*, pp. 207–208.
[34] Weinberg, *A World At Arms*, p. 891.
[35] Craig, *The Fall of Japan*, pp. 181–201; Hasegawa, *Racing the Enemy*, pp. 241–248.
[36] Weinberg, *A World At Arms*, p. 891.

taking the toll of many innocent lives." Indicative of the place of the atomic bombs in forcing the Japanese surrender he continued that "should We continue to fight, it would . . . result in an ultimate collapse and obliteration of the Japanese nation."[37] The next day an imperial cease-fire order to all the Japanese armed forces was issued, and Emperor Hirohito enlisted the support of family members, like his brother Prince Yakamatsu, to ensure that the various Army and Navy commands obeyed. So Japan's troops, which still occupied most of East Asia, lay down their weapons in a process that the attacks on Hiroshima and Nagasaki facilitated. Ironically, as Sadao Asada persuasively has clarified, the Japanese military who had insisted on "a fight to the finish" now "accepted surrender partly because the atomic bomb paradoxically helped them save 'face.'" They could blame the humiliation of surrender on "America's scientific prowess" rather than on their defeat in battle.[38] The formal surrender came on the battleship USS *Missouri* on September 2.

Washington probably received some initial news of the Japanese decision to surrender from the MAGIC code breakers, but the first public notification came to Byrnes at midafternoon on August 14 (Washington, D.C., time is thirteen hours behind that of Tokyo) when the U.S. ambassador to Switzerland informed him that Japan's government accepted the terms he had outlined. He rushed to the White House and shared the information with Truman. As the days after August 10 had dragged on without any Japanese response, Truman worried that he might be forced to resort again to an atomic attack. On August 14, just a few hours before Byrnes arrived with the much-awaited news, Truman expressed his dismay at the Japanese refusal to surrender when he met with the Duke of Windsor and the British Charge d'Affaires Jock Balfour. According to Balfour's dispatch back to London the president also "remarked sadly that he now had no alternative but to order an atomic bomb dropped on Tokyo."[39] Such an awful prospect was soon forgotten, however, when at 6:00 P.M. the Swiss charge d'affaires in Washington delivered the formal and official acceptance to the surrender terms to the secretary of state, who immediately took the news to the president.

By 7:00 P.M. Truman gathered in his office his wife, the service chiefs, and most cabinet members to make the news official. He also made a

---

[37] For Butow's comments and Hirohito's address see *Japan's Decision to Surrender*, pp. 2–3.

[38] See Sadao Asada, "The Shock of the Atomic Bomb," p. 506.

[39] Balfour quoted in Barton J. Berstein, "Conclusion" in Tsuyoshi Hasegawa, *The End of the Pacific War: Reappraisals* (Stanford, 2007), p. 228.

special effort to include the former secretary of state, Cordell Hull, who had received the Japanese declaration of war following the Pearl Harbor attack and who counseled tough surrender terms right to the end. There in the Oval Office before the White House press corps, amidst the flashing of camera bulbs and under the blazing klieg lights for the newsreel cameras, the president advised of the Japanese reply. He deemed it "a full acceptance of the Potsdam Declaration which specifies the unconditional surrender of Japan." He also announced that arrangements were progressing for the formal surrender and Gen. Douglas MacArthur's appointment as Supreme Allied Commander (SCAP) to receive that surrender.[40]

Rumors of the Japanese surrender had been circulating throughout the afternoon and crowds had gathered in front of the White House.

PHOTO 13. Truman reading the announcement of Japanese surrender, August 14, 1945. James F. Byrnes and Adm. William D. Leahy are seated beside him. Franklin Roosevelt's portrait is in the background. (Courtesy Harry S. Truman Presidential Library.)

[40] This account along with the text of Truman's statement is drawn from Truman's *Year of Decisions*, pp. 480–482.

Harry and Bess Truman, hardly the most charismatic occupants of that storied residence, walked to the north lawn and greeted the gathered throng. Truman even allowed himself to flash "a V sign in the manner of Churchill," which brought cheers from the overjoyed and celebrating assembly. A more flamboyant politician might have played more to this spontaneous audience, but Harry Truman retreated back into the White House simply content to call his elderly mother back in Missouri and to report to Eleanor Roosevelt that the promise her husband made following the Pearl Harbor attack had been kept. Yet, at eight o'clock he appeared on the north portico and this time shared some words with the crowd that had chanted: "we want Truman." He told his fellow citizens, "This is a great day, the day we've been waiting for. This is the day we've been looking forward for since December 7, 1941." Then, in words that suggest not only a desire to give the crowd what it needed to hear, but also a continuing naiveté, he idealistically proclaimed that "this is the day for free

PHOTO 14. Harry and Bess Truman wave to the cheering crowd that gathered in front of the White House after the announcement of the Japanese surrender on August 14, 1945. (Courtesy National Archives.)

governments in the world. This is the day that fascism and police government ceases in the world."[41]

Franklin Roosevelt assuredly would have expressed the same sentiment.
Two weeks later in his radio address to the American people on the formal
signing of the surrender documents in Tokyo Bay, Truman paid tribute to
"our departed gallant leader, Franklin D. Roosevelt," whom he described
as the "defender of democracy, [and] architect of world peace and cooperation."[42] Having suddenly been forced to take on FDR's mantle, Harry
Truman had led his nation and its allies to victory over Nazism and
Japanese militarism.

Around the United States from Times Square in New York City to the
smallest towns in the west and the south, Americans joined in the victory
celebration. Two days of public holidays provided time for the celebration,

PHOTO 15. Japan surrenders on the USS *Missouri*, September 2, 1945. (Courtesy
Harry S. Truman Presidential Library.)

[41] Truman, *Year of Decisions*, p. 482.
[42] Truman's radio address, September 1, 1945, *Public Papers of the President: Harry
S. Truman, 1945*, p. 256.

PHOTO 16. Gen. Douglas MacArthur signs the surrender document on board the USS *Missouri*, September 2, 1945. (Courtesy Harry S. Truman Presidential Library.)

although neither could be officially termed V-J day because the official surrender had yet to occur. In Washington, as Stanley Weintraub noted, "priorities shifted to conversion to peace." Announcements and new orders were issued in rapid succession and several snafus occurred, including an executive order authorizing time-and-a-half pay for the two-day holiday, which Truman had to reverse![43] No wonder he wrote to his mother on August 17 that "things have been in such a dizzy whirl here." Mistakes had been made and everyone had been "going at a terrific gait," but he hoped that "we are up with the parade now." Indicating his own expectation that his energies needed to shift to the homefront and the domestic political arena he confided to his "Mamma" that "it is going to be political maneuvers that I have to watch."[44]

---

[43] Weintraub provides details in *The Last Great Victory*, p. 642.
[44] Truman to Mamma and Mary, August 17, 1945, in Ferrell, ed., *Off the Record*, p. 62.

Truman's announcement of Japan's defeat set off deep and heartfelt celebrations among American soldiers, sailors, and airmen in the Pacific theater and among those in Europe preparing to transfer there.[45] They would not have to risk their lives in the feared invasion of Japan. Instead they could return to their homes and resume their peacetime lives. Rather than fighting the 5,400,000 men who remained in the Japanese army and the 1,800,000 serving in the navy, the Allied soldiers instead prepared to accept their surrender.[46] Furthermore, as Weinberg has noted, "the surrender obviated Japanese plans to slaughter Allied prisoners of war as fighting approached the camps where they were held, a project for which considerable preparations had evidently been made, to the horror of prisoners who had already suffered enormously."[47] Truman justifiably could claim that his actions to end the war had saved American lives.

One nation, however, which showed no desire to quit the fighting was the Soviet Union. On August 15, Truman provided for Stalin a copy of the initial SCAP order that set forth basic procedures and arrangements for the occupation. Stalin immediately proposed that the Soviets enlarge their realm by occupying northern Hokkaido. On August 18 Truman rejected this out of hand, but this did not stop the Soviet's theater commander, Marshal Vasilevski, from seeking Moscow's permission to seize the island before a surrender could be made to American troops. Fortuitously for the long-term good of the people of Hokkaido, continued Japanese resistance on Sakhalin, which was to be the launching point for a Soviet attack on Hokkaido, slowed any Soviet military operations. On August 22 Stalin ordered Vasilevski to back off. In forcing this action, Richard Frank holds Truman's "firm reply" of August 18 as being "crucial."[48] But this episode, rarely emphasized these days by American historians, suggests the clear intention of the Soviets to occupy as much as possible of the main Japanese islands. Who knows how much they might have procured and at what cost to the Japanese people without the surrender, which the atomic bombs clearly had helped to force.

---

[45] See the classic essay by Paul Fussell, "Hiroshima: A Soldier's View," *The New Republic*, Vol. 185 (August 22, 29, 1981), pp. 26–30.

[46] I take these numbers from Weinberg, *A World at Arms*, p. 892.

[47] Weinberg, *A World at Arms*, p. 892. Sadly, the surrender did not prevent all killing of American POWs. On August 15 at Fukuoka, officers of the Japanese Western Army Headquarters brutally executed 16 B-29 crew members. See Craig, *The Fall of Japan*, pp. 214–215, for the ghastly details.

[48] Frank, *Downfall*, pp. 323–324. This paragraph relies on Frank's crucial work. Also see the fine work of Tsuyoshi Hasegawa on this subject in *Racing the Enemy*, pp. 252–289.

CHAPTER 7

Necessary, But Was It Right?

In the nineteen fifties, Gen. George C. Marshall, army chief of staff during World War II and the great "organizer of victory," sat for a series of interviews with his biographer, Forrest C. Pogue. Asked about the necessity of dropping the atomic bombs, Marshall replied that "I think it was quite necessary to drop the bombs in order to shorten the war." He explained that "what they [the Japanese] needed was shock action, and they got it. I think it was very wise to use it."[1] Marshall took no pleasure in their use but the distinguished soldier–statesman correctly understood that the two terrible weapons had forced the Japanese surrender when it occurred. By July of 1945 the Japanese had been subjected to months of devastating attacks by B-29s, their capital and other major cities had suffered extensive damage, and the home islands were subjected to a naval blockade that made food and fuel increasingly scarce. The Japanese military and civilian losses had reached approximately three million and there seemed no end in sight. Despite all this, however, Japan's leaders and especially its military clung to notions of *Ketsu-Go*, to a plan that involved inflicting such punishment on the invader in defense of the homeland that the invader would sue for terms. Even after Hiroshima, Nagasaki, and the Soviet attack in Manchuria the military still wanted to pursue that desperate option, but Hirohito broke the impasse in the Japanese government and ordered surrender. He came to understand that the atomic bomb undermined "the fundamental premise" of *Ketsu-Go* "that the United States would have to invade Japan to secure a

[1] Larry Bland, ed., *George C. Marshall Interviews and Reminiscences for Forrest C. Pogue* (Lexington, VA, 1991), pp. 424–425.

decision" in the war.[2] Ultimately, the atomic bombs allowed the emperor and the peace faction in the Japanese government to negotiate an end to the war.[3] George Marshall portrayed the matter correctly. The atomic bombs brought an end to the war in the Pacific.

Writers engaging in wishful thinking and fanciful recreations have sought to fashion circumstances in which the atomic bombs might be seen as unnecessary (and then as almost certainly wrong and immoral). Yet the painful reality that fair-minded observers must concede is that Japan most certainly would have fought on considerably longer unless the United States and its allies had accepted major changes to its Potsdam surrender terms. "Those insisting that Japan's surrender could have been procured without recourse to atomic bombs," Richard Frank noted, "cannot point to any credible evidence from the eight men who effectively controlled Japan's destiny."[4] The Japanese scholar Sadao Asada made essentially the same point in concluding that "given the intransigence of the Japanese military, there were few 'missed opportunities' for earlier peace and that the alternatives available to President Truman in the summer of 1945 were limited."[5] Of course, it is clear that the United States eventually could have defeated Japan without the atomic bomb, but one must appreciate that all the alternate scenarios to secure victory – continued obliteration bombing of Japanese cities and infrastructure, a choking blockade, the terrible invasions – would have meant significantly greater Allied casualties and much higher Japanese civilian and military casualties.[6]

Those who rush to judge Truman's decision to use the atomic bombs must hesitate a little to appreciate that had he not authorized the attacks on Hiroshima and Nagasaki thousands of American and Allied soldiers, sailors, marines, and airmen would have been added to the lists of those killed in World War II. This would have included not only those involved in the planned invasions of the home islands but also American, British, and Australian ground forces in Southeast Asia and the Southwest Pacific

---

[2] Frank, *Downfall*, p. 348.
[3] Sadao Asada discussed this well in his "The Shock of the Atomic Bomb and Japan's Decision to Surrender," pp. 496–497.
[4] Frank referred to the Big Six, Baron Kido, and Emperor Hirohito. See, *Downfall*, p. 343.
[5] Asada, "The Shock of the Atomic Bomb and Japan's Decision to Surrender," p. 512.
[6] See the thoughtful consideration of "alternatives" in Barton J. Bernstein, "Understanding the Atomic Bomb and the Japanese Surrender: Missed Opportunities, Little-Known Near Disasters, and Modern Memory," *Diplomatic History*, Vol. 19 (Spring, 1995), pp. 236–259.

who expected to engage the Japanese in bloody fighting in the months preceding such assaults. Added to their number would have been the thousands of Allied prisoners of war whom the Japanese planned to execute. Could an American president have survived politically and personally knowing that he might have used a weapon that could have avoided their slaughter? To further complicate the rush to judgment one must acknowledge that Truman was likely correct in March, 1958 when he told Tsukasa Nitoguri, the chairman of the Hiroshima City Council, that the atomic bombs prevented a quarter of a million Japanese deaths in an invasion.[7] Hard as it may be to accept when one sees the visual record of the terrible destruction of Hiroshima and Nagasaki, Japanese losses probably would have been substantially greater without the atomic bombs. Furthermore, the atomic attacks changed the whole dynamic of the occupation of Japan. Ironically, they facilitated a quick and easy surrender and a broadly cooperative populace in a way that no other method of military victory could have guaranteed.

Moreover, the use of the awful weapons abruptly ended the death and suffering of innocent third parties among peoples throughout Asia. Rather surprisingly, the enormous wartime losses of the Chinese, Koreans, Filipinos, Vietnamese, and Javanese at the hands of the Japanese receive little attention in weighing the American effort to shock the Japanese into surrender. The losses in Hiroshima and Nagasaki assuredly were horrific, but they pale in significance when compared to the estimates of seventeen to twenty-four million deaths attributed to the Japanese during their rampage from Manchuria to New Guinea.[8] Gavan Daws accurately described "Asia under the Japanese" as "a charnel house of atrocities."[9] During the months of war following the attack on Pearl Harbor, reliable estimates establish that between 200,000 and 300,000 persons died each month either directly or indirectly at Japanese hands. Furthermore, Robert Newman tellingly reveals that "the last months were in many ways the worst; starvation and disease aggravated the usual beatings, beheadings, and battle deaths. It is plausible to hold that upward of 250,000 people,

---

[7] Truman's letter of March 12, 1958 in response to the critical resolution of the Hiroshima City Council in Truman Papers, PPF, Box 20.

[8] The lower estimate is taken from Robert P. Newman, *Truman and the Hiroshima Cult*, pp. 138–139. The upper estimate is from Werner Gruhl, *Imperial Japan's World War Two, 1931–1945* (New Brunswick, NJ, 2007), pp. 18–22, 203–205.

[9] Daws quoted in Newman, *Truman and the Hiroshima Cult*, p. 138.

mostly Asian but some Westerners, *would have died each month the Japanese Empire struggled in its death throes beyond July 1945.*"[10]

If the atomic bombs shortened the war, averted the need for a land invasion, saved countless more lives on both sides of the ghastly conflict than it cost, and brought to an end the Japanese brutalization of the conquered peoples of Asia, does this make their use moral? From the outset some Americans have answered in the negative. Even some of those involved in devising military strategy during World War II eventually came to criticize the use of the atomic bombs. Admiral Leahy, a perennial skeptic about the utility of the atomic bomb, later blasted the use of what he refused to call a bomb or an explosive, but described as "a poisonous thing that kills people by its deadly radioactive reaction, more than by the explosive force it develops." In his memoir published in 1950 Leahy expressed his sentiment that "in being the first to use it we had adopted an ethical standard common to the barbarians of the Dark Ages." The old admiral noted that he "was not taught to make war in that fashion," and then asserted that "wars cannot be won by destroying women and children." Using these "new and terrible instruments of uncivilized warfare," represented for him "a modern type of barbarism not worthy of Christian man."[11]

Such retrospective castigations could be replicated with quotations from other wartime luminaries like Generals MacArthur and Eisenhower, yet it is important to note that no military officials counseled the president against using the weapons *prior* to Hiroshima.[12] He had acted with the advice and full support of his chief civilian and military advisers and with the unequivocal endorsement of his British allies. The consensus view held that the atomic bombs were legitimate weapons of war. Margaret Gowing, the historian of the British Atomic Energy Authority, reminded her readers during the nineteen sixties that the weapons used in 1945 "were regarded primarily as super explosives, as an economical means of delivering the equivalent of a massive quantity of T.N.T."[13] While the American policy makers hoped that the impressive power of such a single weapon might shock the Japanese into capitulation, the estimates of the power and destructive force of the new weapon varied considerably, and there was no full appreciation of the dastardly impact of the lethal

---

[10] Newman, *Truman and the Hiroshima Cult*, p. 139. (Italics in the original.)
[11] William D. Leahy, *I Was There* (New York, 1950), pp. 441–442.
[12] See Robert James Maddox, ed., *Hiroshima in History*, pp. 14–22.
[13] Margaret Gowing, *Britain and Atomic Energy, 1939–1945*, p. 381.

radiation that a nuclear explosion generated. Indicative of the latter, General George Marshall even planned to utilize atomic bombs as battlefield weapons in the projected invasion of Kyushu, and to move American troops through the targeted areas right after the explosions.[14] Such was the limited knowledge about the new weapon prior to its use against Japan.

It was not military men but religious representatives who mounted the strongest and most sustained moral critique of the American use of the atomic bombs. Samuel McCrea Cavert, the general secretary of the Federal Council of the Churches of Christ of America, led the way on August 9 when he protested to Truman about the "indiscriminate" nature of the atomic bombing.[15] Harry Truman chose not to avoid facing such criticisms of his actions. On August 11 he responded to Cavert and admitted that "nobody is more disturbed over the use of [a]tomic bombs than I am." Yet he went further in his own defense and explained "but I was greatly disturbed by the unwarranted attack by the Japanese on Pearl Harbor and their murder of our prisoners of war." Indicative of his frame of mind as he waited for Japan's surrender he clarified for Cavert that "the only language they seem to understand is the one we have been using to bombard them. When you have to deal with a beast you have to treat him as a beast. It is most regrettable," he acknowledged, "but nevertheless true."[16] Fire, it seemed to him, needed to be countered with even greater fire. Long after the war ended, he regularly reacted to critics of the atomic bomb – whom he once referred to (in a letter to Eleanor Roosevelt of all people) as "sob sisters" – by sneering at their failure to criticize the Japanese attack on Pearl Harbor and "the murders committed there." It revealed to him a "double standard of morality." He regularly reassured himself that while the critics assailed him "the men who were on the ground doing their jobs share my opinion that their lives and the lives of a half million other youngsters were saved by dropping the bomb."[17] In April 1962 the former president defended his action with a similar argument in a letter he drafted but never sent to the diplomatic historian Herbert Feis. Describing the inquisitive Feis as "like the usual egghead," he went on to forcefully note that it was "a great thing that you or any other

---

[14] Marc Gallicchio, "After Nagasaki: General Marshall's Plan for Tactical Nuclear Weapons in Japan," *Prologue*, Vol. 23 (Winter, 1991), pp. 396–404.

[15] Cavert to Truman, August 9, 1945, in Robert H. Ferrell, ed., *Harry S. Truman and the Bomb: A Documentary History* (Worland, WY, 1996), pp. 71–72.

[16] Truman to Cavert, August 11, 1945, in Ferrell, ed., *Harry S. Truman and the Bomb*, p. 72.

[17] Truman to Eleanor Roosevelt, August 7, 1959, Truman Papers, PPF, Box 509.

contemplator 'after the fact' didn't have to make the decision. Our boys would all be dead."[18] The unsent note reflected his true feelings.

Truman's firm conviction that he had done the necessary thing in dropping the bomb, thus ending the war and saving numerous lives in the process, did not stave off his serious moral qualms about the action. On the day after the bombing of Nagasaki he told his cabinet of his order that no more atomic bombs be dropped. In words that reveal his personal anguish and his growing recognition that Hiroshima and Nagasaki were much more than military targets, he explained that "the thought of wiping out another 100,000 people is horrible." As Secretary of Commerce Henry Wallace recorded in his diary, "he [Truman] didn't like the idea of killing, as he said, 'all those kids.'"[19] Truman's experience in August of 1945 deeply colored his whole attitude to nuclear weapons. He never again spoke of them as military weapons to which the United States could make easy resort and indicated some retreat from his pre-Hiroshima view that the atomic bomb was "just" another military weapon. At the time of the Berlin blockade crisis in July, 1948 when certain advisers sought the transfer of atomic weapons from civilian to military control he refused their request and explained: "I don't think we ought to use this thing [the atomic bomb] unless we absolutely have to.... You have got to understand that this isn't a military weapon.... It is used to wipe out women and children and unarmed people, and not for military uses. So we have got to treat this differently from rifles and cannon and ordinary things like that."[20] In a post-Hiroshima world Truman understood what he had not completely grasped in 1945. In his farewell address in January 1953 the president held that "starting an atomic war is totally unthinkable for rational men." When questioned on his address by Atomic Energy Commissioner Thomas E. Murray, who spoke to the "morality of atomic warfare," Truman responded bluntly that using the atomic bomb was "far worse than gas or biological warfare because it affects the civilian population and murders them by wholesale."[21]

Truman, however, hardly became a nuclear pacifist. He understood that the United States must maintain its nuclear capability and, indeed, must be willing to use it if need be. In May, 1948 the president received

[18] Truman to Feis, late April, 1962, in Poen, ed., *Strictly Personal and Confidential*, p. 34.
[19] John Morton Blum, ed., *The Price of Vision: The Diary of Henry A. Wallace, 1942–1946* (Boston, 1973), p. 474.
[20] Diary entry for July 21, 1948, *Journals of David Lilienthal*, Vol. II, p. 391.
[21] See the exchange of letters between Murray and Truman, January, 1953 in Truman Papers, PSF, Box 112.

briefings on atomic tests on Eniwetok Atoll from AEC Chairman David Lilienthal. In the course of their conversation Truman referred to Hiroshima and Nagasaki and told the AEC chief that "I don't want to have to do that again, ever." And yet, while he encouraged Lilienthal to pursue atomic energy for peaceful and constructive purposes, he made clear that the weapons must stay. "Until we are sure about peace, there's nothing else to do," he concluded.[22] The following year he again conversed with Lilienthal and acknowledged that the atomic bomb "isn't just another weapon" but he nonetheless pledged, "we will never use it again if we can possibly help it."[23] And, even during the Berlin blockade crisis when he refused to surrender the bomb into the hands of the military, he told Secretary of Defense James Forrestal that "he prayed he would never have to make such a decision again, but if it became necessary, no one need have a misgiving but [that] he would do so."[24]

A continuing recognition that he might in some future terrible circumstance be called upon again to use atomic weapons never removed Truman's angst about the two bombings he did authorize. In his final weeks in office Truman attended a dinner in honor of Winston Churchill at the British embassy in Washington, D.C. Reveling in being Britain's prime minister once again, and no doubt eager to stimulate a lively evening, Churchill asked Truman "whether he would have his answer ready when they both stood before Saint Peter to account for their part in dropping atomic bombs on Japan."[25] The question clearly troubled the president and the other dinner companions had to move the conversation quickly in other directions. Truman obviously didn't appreciate discussions of guilt or innocence however much they might be mixed with cigars, port, and Churchill's company. Perhaps they cut this normal man too close to the quick. When Los Alamos Laboratory Director J. Robert Oppenheimer met the president in late 1945 and told him that he believed that he had blood on his hands, Truman reacted angrily. He recalled telling the now famous physicist that "the blood is on my hands. Let me worry

---

[22] Lilienthal, *Journals of David Lilienthal*, Vol. II, p. 342. David S. Broscious concluded that "Truman viewed the use of nuclear weapons with great solemnity." See Broscious, "Longing for International Control, Banking on American Superiority: Harry S. Truman's Approach to Nuclear Weapons," in John Lewis Gaddis et al., eds., *Cold War Statesmen Confront the Bomb*, p. 20.

[23] Lilienthal, *Journals of David Lilienthal*, Vol. II, p. 474.

[24] Millis, ed., *The Forrestal Diaries*, p. 487.

[25] See the account in Dean G. Acheson, *Present at the Creation: My Years in the State Department* (New York, 1969), pp. 715–716.

about that." The president later reportedly told his undersecretary of state, Dean Acheson, that "I don't want to see that son-of-a-bitch in this office ever again."[26] It would seem that Oppenheimer had touched a raw nerve.

If Truman had blood on his hands, which the evidence suggests he worried about, he hardly stood alone among the participants in the enormous, ghastly struggle that came to be known as World War II. Well over fifty million people lost their lives in that gigantic conflict, which descended to new lows of barbarism in both European and Pacific theaters. Restraints that previously had directed soldiers to spare noncombatants were thrown off. Barton Bernstein has observed insightfully that "the older morality crumbled in the crucible of what became virtually total war." In this "emerging conception of nearly total war," Bernstein explained further, "the enemy was not simply soldiers but non-combatants. They worked in factories, ran the economy, maintained the civic life, constituted much of the nation, and were the core of national cohesion. Kill them, and soon production would tumble, the national fabric would rip, armies would soon feel homeless, and the government might surrender."[27] Merely listing such cities as Shanghai, Nanking, Leningrad, Rotterdam, Coventry, London, Hamburg, Dresden, and Tokyo makes the point. As a number of writers have noted succinctly, a "moral Rubicon" had been crossed long before Hiroshima and Nagasaki.[28] Indiscriminate bombing had become the norm for the Anglo-American forces well before 1945. In fact, as William Hitchcock has revealed, even the heroic liberation of Western Europe resulted in a grisly catalogue of civilian casualties among the very peoples the Allies aimed to free from Nazi oppression.[29] Suffering from saturation bombing was widespread. By 1945, Stimson's biographer noted, "the sheer scale of the frightfulness inflicted by the Nazis in Europe and in Russia and by the Japanese in China had hardened military

---

[26] On this episode see Kai Bird and Martin Sherwin, *American Prometheus: The Triumph and Tragedy of J. Robert Oppenheimer* (New York, 2005), p. 332. As Bird and Sherwin note, Truman embellished this story over the years. In the most celebrated version of the encounter Truman reportedly gave Oppenheimer his handkerchief and asked him if he would like to wipe the blood off. On this also see Paul Boyer, *By the Bomb's Early Light: American Thought and Culture at the Dawn of the Atomic Age* (Chapel Hill, NC, 1994), p. 193; and David McCullough, *Truman*, p. 475.

[27] Bernstein, "Understanding the Bomb and the Japanese Surrender," pp. 259–260.

[28] See Frank, *Downfall*, pp. 46–47. Also see on this broad point Ronald Schaffer, *Wings of Judgment*; and Michael Sherry, *The Rise of American Air Power: The Creation of Armageddon* (New Haven, CT, 1987), pp. 256–316.

[29] William I. Hitchcock, *The Bitter Road to Freedom: A New History of the Liberation of Europe* (New York, 2008), pp. 21–22, 29–30.

hearts and relaxed military consciences."[30] Churchill and Roosevelt both approved the brutal endeavors to break the morale of their foes, which they hoped ultimately would secure victory and save lives. The Tokyo fire bombings took place on FDR's watch after all.[31]

Surprisingly, however, in the moral assessments of the war Churchill and FDR escape the condemnation heaped on Harry Truman. This is doubtless in significant part because Hiroshima and Nagasaki became the focus of so much attention. John Hersey's powerful and emotionally challenging *Hiroshima*, which first appeared in the *New Yorker* in 1946, began the trend and it hasn't really stopped. The American bombings became the subject of extensive dissection and analysis. But in all of this, as the historian Morton Keller angrily noted around the fiftieth anniversary of Hiroshima, most critics "ignore[d] the character of the Japanese regime that brought war to the Pacific." He deemed this the "equivalent of discussing the end of the European war by dwelling on the bombing of Dresden while saying little about the Nazi regime."[32] Rarely given the attention accorded Hitler's dastardly attempt to exterminate the Jewish people, the vast Japanese atrocities throughout Asia surface hardly at all in the analyses of Truman's critics. Perhaps some of those fixated on Hiroshima and Nagasaki might spare at least some thought for the vast numbers of innocent victims of Japanese aggression before they rush to judgment.

Truman's accusers might also refrain from putting him in some singular dock of history at least until they carefully consider the responsibility of the Japanese leadership for the fate of their own people. Postwar Japanese leaders effectively played up their victim role to induce a certain guilt among Americans about the war's ending. This helped disguise the important reality explained by Herbert Bix that "it was not so much the Allied policy of unconditional surrender that prolonged the Pacific war, as it was the unrealistic and incompetent actions of Japan's highest leaders. Blinded by their preoccupation with the fate of the imperial house, those leaders let pass every opportunity to end the lost war until it was too late."[33] In moral terms surely the Japanese leadership had a responsibility to surrender at least by June of 1945, when there existed no reasonable prospect of success and when their civilian population suffered so greatly. Instead, the twisted neo-*samurai* who led the Japanese military geared up with true *banzai*

---

[30] Godfrey Hodgson, *The Colonel*, p. 278.
[31] On casualties from this raid see Frank, *Downfall*, p. 18.
[32] Morton Keller, "Amnesia Day," *The New Republic*, Issues 4209–4210 (September 18, 25, 1995), p. 14.
[33] Bix, "Japan's Delayed Surrender," p. 223.

spirit to engage the whole population in a kind of national *kamikaze* campaign. Their stupidity and perfidy in perpetrating and prolonging the war should not be ignored.

After all this, must we still ask was it right? Must we still wrestle with the morality of the atomic bomb? Certainly Harry Truman hardly spent much time on the moral aspects of the matter *before* the bombings. He deemed the bombs to be legitimate weapons of war and the decision to use them required no tortured agonizing for him, a reality aided by his refraining from seriously probing the "military" nature of the targets. He hoped that the bombs would end the war and secure peace with the fewest American casualties and so they did. Surely he took the action that any American president would have undertaken. Perhaps the effort to evaluate his action retrospectively in explicit moral terms is insufficient. Should there be a distinction between the "moral" aspects of Truman's decision and the "political-military" quality of it? The much maligned and misunderstood political genius Niccolo Machiavelli would certainly have thought so.

In his advice to the magnificent Lorenzo d'Medici, the brilliant Florentine political philosopher pointed to the harshness and evil in the world and observed that "a man who wants to make a profession of good in all regards must come to ruin among so many who are not good." Hence, he counseled that "it is necessary to a prince, if he wants to maintain himself [and his state], to learn to be able not to be good, and to use this and not use it according to necessity."[34] At times he must explicitly turn his back on religiously based morality because the prince "cannot observe all those things for which men are held good, since he is often under a necessity, to maintain his state, of acting against faith, against charity, against humanity, against religion." For Machiavelli, the prince, in order to secure his state, "must not depart from good, when possible, but know how to enter into evil, when forced by necessity."[35] Isaiah Berlin in his astute commentary on Machiavelli summed up the argument well: "One can save one's soul, or one can found or maintain or serve a great and glorious state; but not always both at once."[36] In an imperfect world, Berlin interprets Machiavelli as conveying, "force and guile must be met with force and guile."[37]

[34] Niccolo Machiavelli, *The Prince*, translated and introduced by Harvey C. Mansfield, 2nd ed. (Chicago, 1998), p. 61.

[35] Machiavelli, *The Prince*, p. 70. (Note the discussion in Chapter 18 in particular.)

[36] Isaiah Berlin, "The Originality of Machiavelli," in his *Against the Current: Essays in the History of Ideas*, ed. Henry Hardy (New York, 1980), p. 50.

[37] Berlin, "The Originality of Machiavelli," p. 51.

Harry Truman rarely, if ever, thought of himself in the same category as Lorenzo d'Medici, nor did he classify himself with Cesare Borgia and the other case studies of *The Prince*. It's likely he would have described anyone who referred to Machiavelli in discussing his actions as an "egghead" like Herbert Feis. Yet clearly reasons of state motivated Truman and Stimson and Byrnes and their military advisers. In retrospect within the privacy of his own heart and soul it is likely that Truman understood he had been forced by necessity to enter into evil. And, so indeed, he had. He ordered the bombing of cities in which thousands of noncombatants, among them the innocent elderly and the sick, women and children, were annihilated. Evaluated in isolation, each atomic bombing assuredly was a deeply immoral act deserving of condemnation. The fact that it did the least harm possible of the available options to gain victory, and that it brought an end to destruction, death, and casualties on an even more massive scale cannot obviate this, although it might satisfy those who accept a utilitarian approach to morality in which good ends can serve to justify certain immoral means.

The British philosopher Elizabeth Anscombe assuredly did not subscribe to such a "consequentialist" point of view. In 1956, while serving as a research fellow of Somerville College at Oxford University, she objected to Harry Truman's being awarded an honorary degree by her much celebrated institution because he had authorized the use of the atomic bombs. The following year she published a pamphlet entitled *Mr. Truman's Degree* in which she laid forth the basis for her objection in an argument that Robert Newman rightly has termed "strong on emotion and lamentably weak on its historical claims."[38] Anscombe, a scholar of profound integrity, held with passionate commitment that in bombing Hiroshima and Nagasaki "it was certainly decided to kill the innocent as a means to an end." For her, this was "always murder" and obviously wrong. Her view has proved decidedly influential in subsequent decades. Yet, Anscombe wrongly presented a Japan "desirous of negotiating peace" and inaccurately suggested that if the Allies had overcome their "fixation on unconditional surrender" the war might have been brought to a quick end. She failed to consider that the very altering of the surrender terms might have been interpreted by the Japanese military hardliners as confirmation of their analysis regarding Western weakness that underlay the *Ketsu-Go* strategy. In fact, it might then have led to a substantial prolongation of the war during which Japanese atrocities throughout Asia and Allied obliteration bombing of Japan, both of which involved

---

[38] Newman, *Truman and the Hiroshima Cult*, p. 124.

enormous killing of innocents, would have continued. Anscombe ultimately argued that in light of Truman's actions the principle of "doing evil that good may come" should be reformulated as "every fool can be as much of a knave as suits him."[39]

Truman was neither a fool nor a knave. He was a serious Baptist who tried to live by a moral code grounded, as he later explained, in the twentieth chapter of the Book of Exodus (the Ten Commandments) and the Sermon on the Mount.[40] He was not an amoral or immoral man who could blithely ignore the fifth commandment's instruction: "Thou shall not kill." Truman instead sought to link himself to the beatitudes preached by Jesus in his famous sermon. He wanted to be numbered among the "peacemakers" of the world who would be blessed. He later stated honestly: "I abhor war and I am opposed to any kind of killing – whether by atomic bomb or bow and arrow."[41] Truman was, however, also a person who knew that decisions in the sometimes confusing fog of war placed the policy maker in circumstances where he sometimes had neither a clear nor easy moral option. Perhaps Truman had himself and the atomic bomb decision retrospectively in mind when he wrote fifteen years after their use in a discourse on decision making that "sometimes you have a choice of evils, in which case you try to take the course that is likely to bring the least harm."[42]

From the perspective of over six decades Truman's use of the bomb, when viewed in the context of the long and terrible war, should be seen as his choosing the lesser of the evils available to him. Admittedly, he did not weigh carefully the options in a careful moral calculus at the time and proceed forward with that understanding, but fair-minded observers will see that he chose what might be termed a necessary evil. Henry L. Stimson had it exactly right when he wrote in 1947 that "the decision to use the atomic bomb was a decision that brought death to over a hundred thousand Japanese. No explanation can change that fact and I do not wish to gloss over it. But this deliberate, premeditated destruction was our least abhorrent choice."[43] "Abhorrent," for sure, but it must be understood, the "least abhorrent" as well so as to bring the bloodshed to an end. Truman,

---

[39] G. E. M. Anscombe's "Mr. Truman's Degree" reprinted in *The Collected Philosophical Papers of G. E. M. Anscombe*, Vol. III, *Ethics, Religion and Politics* (Oxford: Blackwell, 1981), pp. 62–71.

[40] Truman later outlined his religious outlook in his *Mr. Citizen* (New York, 1960), pp. 127–141; see especially pp. 134–136.

[41] Truman, *Mr. Citizen*, p. 267.   [42] Truman, *Mr. Citizen*, p. 263.

[43] Henry L. Stimson, "The Decision to Use the Atomic Bomb," *Harper's*, Vol. 194 (February, 1947), pp. 97–107; quotation from p. 107.

along with many others, has blood on his hands but he also stopped the veritable flood of blood on all sides. The reality that he prevented much greater bloodshed must be acknowledged. So too must it be appreciated that he did not turn his back on some feasible moral course of action that would have secured a Japanese surrender.

As future anniversaries of the dropping of the atomic bombs on Hiroshima and Nagasaki occur, one might hope for less moralizing condemnation of Truman's decision until the critics specify at least a less immoral and yet still feasible course of action to end the terrible war. Perhaps there might even be some empathy for the man who felt required to make the decision and who carried the burden of it. Harry Truman of Independence, Missouri, was hardly some moral monster who now needs to be placed retrospectively on trial for war crimes. Those who from the safe distance of sixty-five years criticize his decision would do well to place themselves in his shoes and ask what they might have done in the circumstances.[44] Perhaps they might also ask if the weapon had been ready say a year before would they have refrained from using it against Hitler's Berlin where they might have wiped out the viperous head of the Nazi regime and possibly saved the lives of millions on the battlefields and in the gas ovens. Or, instead, perhaps they simply might pray, if they be so inclined, that leaders in our own time and in the future are never forced by horrible circumstances to make such decisions.

---

[44] This observation draws on John Lewis Gaddis, *Surprise, Security, and the American Experience* (Cambridge, MA, 2004), p. 33.

CHAPTER 8

Byrnes, the Soviets, and the American Atomic Monopoly

Harry S. Truman and James F. Byrnes had little time to catch their breath as World War II ended. Pressures and demands came at them relentlessly, and they developed policies concerning the atomic bomb in circumstances where they juggled numerous other serious issues. Over the coming months and without any formal decision, Truman gravitated more to domestic politics and policies while Byrnes saw himself as the main player in the foreign policy domain. Truman hardly seemed perturbed by the division. The president had full confidence in his chosen appointee, and certainly Byrnes played a role in shaping the initial postwar approach to the American atomic monopoly. On this matter, which possessed both domestic and international dimensions, the Americans were mapping new terrain with no set rules or norms to guide them. Understanding the efforts of Truman, Byrnes, and their associates immediately after the use of the atomic bombs is important for clarifying American intentions regarding these weapons and the place they played in postwar American diplomacy. Such an examination reveals that the forceful purpose with which the Americans developed and used the atomic bombs as weapons of war was followed by much less certainty and even confusion as the Truman administration struggled to fashion the role that nuclear weapons and energy should play in the postwar era.

In his powerful August 6 statement announcing the use of the atomic bomb against Hiroshima, Truman concluded by noting that, while it "has never been the habit of the scientists of this country or the policy of this Government to withhold from the world scientific knowledge," the new circumstances regarding atomic energy required a different approach. In what seems, in retrospect, to be an eminently sensible position, the president advised that the United States would not "divulge the technical processes of production or all the military applications, pending further examination of possible methods of protecting us and the rest of the world from the danger of sudden destruction."[1] He promised to gain congressional approval for a commission to control the production and use of atomic power. Three days later in his report on the Potsdam Conference he reiterated this cautious approach and pronounced that "the atomic bomb is too dangerous to be loose in a lawless world." Associating the United States with its Manhattan Project partners, Great Britain and Canada, Truman assured his radio audience that the "secret of its production" would not be revealed "until the means have been found to control the bomb so as to protect ourselves and the rest of the world from the danger of total destruction." He presented the Americans as veritable "trustees of this force" who were obliged "to prevent its misuse, and to turn it into channels of service to mankind." He even expressed a hope that "its power be made an overwhelming influence towards world peace."[2] Such a sincere hope proved difficult to bring to fruition.

A certain haphazard and even contradictory quality characterized the Truman administration's efforts to implement these seemingly cautious initial goals. Despite the Truman assurances that the United States would protect the "secret" of the atomic bomb, just a few days after his Potsdam report and even before the Japanese had surrendered, General Groves released the physicist Henry DeWolf Smyth's official history of the Manhattan Project, *Atomic Energy for Military Purposes*.[3] McGeorge Bundy in his important study of American nuclear policies judged that "the Smyth report contained the most important single set of technical disclosures in the history of nuclear weapons."[4] More recently Michael D. Gordin has argued that the Smyth Report proved useful to the Soviet Union "as a general guide to the problems of building nuclear weapons" because it provided a "road map [which] would accelerate the Soviet

---

[1] Statement by the President Announcing the Use of the A-Bomb at Hiroshima, August 6, 1945, in *Public Papers of the Presidents of the United States: Harry S. Truman, 1945* (Washington, D.C., 1961), pp. 199–200.

[2] Radio Report to the American People on the Potsdam Conference, August 9, 1945, *Truman Public Papers, 1945*, pp. 212–213.

[3] Henry DeWolf Smyth, *Atomic Energy for Military Purposes: The Official Report on the Development of the Atomic Bomb under the Auspices of the United States Government, 1940–45* (Princeton, NJ, 1945).

[4] Bundy, *Danger and Survival*, p. 134.

nuclear program."[5] Such an outcome presumably would have bothered the tough-minded General Groves, but in August 1945 he thought he was allowing for the release only of information that eventually could be discerned by the world scientific community while he simultaneously and implicitly clarified what must remain appropriately classified within the Manhattan Project and whatever body might succeed it.

Secretary of States Byrnes proved much less willing to release information about the atomic bomb. On August 18, George Harrison, Stimson's key aide on nuclear matters showed Byrnes a letter that Robert Oppenheimer had sent to Henry Stimson encouraging immediate initiatives to arrange for international control of the new weapons. Byrnes judged such initiatives as inappropriate at the present moment. He instructed Harrison "to tell Dr. Oppenheimer for the time being his proposal about an international agreement was not practical and that he and the rest of the [Manhattan Project] gang should pursue their work full force."[6] Byrnes had other things higher on his priority list than any hurried action on this matter. Additionally, he hoped that the American monopoly would benefit in some ill-defined way his diplomatic endeavors at an important upcoming meeting.

Byrnes had but a few weeks from the victory over Japan to gear up for the first meeting of the Council of Foreign Ministers (CFM) established at Potsdam, which was scheduled to meet in London in September. Before he departed Washington he made some key changes in the department of state. Most notably, he appointed Dean Acheson to serve as his deputy there. Acheson, at this stage, had nothing of the strong anti-Soviet reputation he would later develop, but he had aligned with Byrnes in supporting tough surrender terms for Japan and had been involved in negotiating the Dumbarton Oaks agreements that lay the groundwork for postwar international cooperation, albeit on American terms.[7] While Byrnes sought Acheson's help to administer the state department, he recruited the Republican foreign policy expert John Foster Dulles to join him at the various CFM meetings. With his eyes set on the domestic political scene, and with prescience concerning "the gradual re-emergence of Congress as

[5] Michael D. Gordin, *Red Cloud at Dawn: Truman, Stalin, and the End of the Atomic Monopoly* (New York, 2009), p. 99.

[6] Memorandum for the Record by George L. Harrison, August 18, 1945, Miscellaneous Historical Documents Collection, Truman Library.

[7] On Acheson and his outlook at this stage see Robert Beisner, "Patterns of Peril: Dean Acheson Joins the Cold Warriors, 1945–46," *Diplomatic History*, Vol. 20 (Summer, 1996), pp. 321–355.

a major influence on the making of foreign policy," Byrnes aimed to ensure that his foreign policy had a bipartisan gloss and that Dulles would assist him in enlisting Republican support for any and all treaties he negotiated.[8] Byrnes intended to be a secretary of state who took the lead in foreign policy formulation within the administration, and, as such, he evidenced no regret at the impending retirement of Secretary of War Henry L. Stimson.

After his distinguished public career culminating in his great service in World War II, Stimson prepared for retirement now that victory had been secured. However, the old man did not plan to go quietly into private life, but rather to influence the Truman administration's direction on policy regarding the atomic bomb. He earlier had tried to tutor Truman about the "master card," which he thought could give the United States important leverage in settling postwar issues. The president in that instance proved an inattentive pupil. Yet Stimson possessed true determination as a teacher and he also displayed a willingness to revise his lecture notes. After the dropping of the atomic bombs and the Japanese surrender Stimson withdrew to a hunting club in the Adirondacks for some much deserved rest. There, in the midst of restoring his physical health, Stimson worried about the meaning of the American atomic monopoly for future international relations. He feared that an American attempt to maintain its monopoly and to apply pressure on the Soviet Union would lead to failure and an arms race.[9] With the aid of Assistant Secretary of War John McCloy, Stimson began to formulate a proposal for the international sharing of atomic information. Here his developing ideas began to conflict directly with the hopes and plans of Jimmy Byrnes.

After visiting with Stimson in the Adirondacks, John McCloy raised their ideas for international sharing of atomic technology with the secretary of state upon his return to Washington. Byrnes's thinking had advanced on a quite different track. He quickly conveyed to McCloy his belief that it would be a long time before the Soviets could catch up with the Americans. Now, with the London CFM on the very near horizon, Byrnes told McCloy that "the Russians were only sensitive to power and all the world, including the Russians, were cognizant of the power of this bomb, and with it in his hip pocket he felt he was in a far better position to come back with tangible accomplishments even if he did not threaten anyone

---

[8] On the reemergence of Congress as a factor in the making of foreign policy see Gaddis, *The United States and the Origins of the Cold War*, pp. 254–263.
[9] See Hodgson, *The Colonel*, pp. 356–361.

expressly with it."[10] Byrnes put essentially the same view to the secretary of war on the elderly statesman's return to the nation's capital. When Stimson raised "how to handle Russia with the big bomb," he claimed that he found that Byrnes "was very much against any attempt to cooperate with Stalin." Stimson confided to his diary that Byrnes's "mind is full of the problems with the coming meeting of the foreign ministers and he looks to having the presence of the bomb in his pocket, so to speak, as a great weapon to get through the thing."[11] Stimson met briefly with Truman and tried to convey his reservations about the Byrnes approach but had little impact. Instead he scheduled a longer meeting at which he would present the memorandum on which he and McCloy still worked. By the time of that meeting Byrnes had left Washington for his London meeting uninhibited by any of Stimson's thinking.

Stimson obviously judged Byrnes's approach regarding the possible diplomatic advantage of the atomic bomb as unseemly and unwise. Yet, given Byrnes's difficult negotiating experience with the Soviets at Potsdam and his long experience as a political operator, it hardly seems surprising that he wanted to enter the London discussions backed by the possible diplomatic weight of the atomic bomb. More surprising than this, however, is how little consideration the Truman administration actually gave to how its possession of the atomic bomb might be exploited diplomatically, especially with regard to the Soviet Union. Byrnes neither commissioned planning documents on this matter nor assigned members of his department to consider potential strategies. In retrospect, the truly astonishing quality about America's atomic monopoly is how little policy makers deliberated about some possible diplomatic advantage. Byrnes personally engaged in mere wishful thinking that the possession of the bomb might assist his negotiating position, while other leading officials like Stimson and McCloy focused from the outset on sharing atomic technology. With all the debate over "atomic diplomacy" this obvious point is rarely stressed. The Truman administration failed to practice atomic diplomacy in a deliberate manner. The atomic bomb was neither used as some kind of stick to coerce the Soviets nor was it offered as some kind of carrot to enlist their cooperation. Of course, whether the United States could have exploited the diplomatic power of the atomic bomb effectively must remain in the realm of speculation. That it didn't try seriously is a matter of historical fact.

---

[10] John McCloy Diary, September 2, 1945, quoted in Kai Bird, *The Chairman: John J. McCloy, The Making of the American Establishment* (New York, 1992), pp. 261–262.
[11] Stimson Diaries, September 4, 1945.

Truman largely left Byrnes to his own devices as the secretary set off for his London meetings. The president, "increasingly preoccupied with domestic conversion," as Alonzo Hamby noted, "appears to have paid only limited attention to diplomacy after Potsdam."[12] Matters such as manpower requirements and the liquidation of war agencies increasingly garnered his interest. Naturally he maintained his responsibilities as head of state and hosted France's President Charles de Gaulle on his visit to Washington in late August. But his specific remarks on foreign policy bore a very general, almost clichéd quality. In a national address to the American people marking the formal surrender of the Japanese to Gen. Douglas MacArthur on board the USS *Missouri* in Tokyo Bay, Truman platitudinously proclaimed that "with the other United Nations we move towards a new and better world of cooperation, of peace and international good will and cooperation."[13] Once in London, Secretary Byrnes soon discovered that cooperation hardly characterized the approach of his Soviet opposite.

The Potsdam protocols established the CFM primarily to oversee the drafting of peace treaties for Germany's defeated European allies such as Italy, Rumania, and Bulgaria and to settle other geopolitical issues. On his way to London on board the *Queen Elizabeth* Byrnes had explained to members of his delegation that "I know how to deal with the Russians. It's just like the U.S. Senate. You build a post office in their state, and they'll build a post office in our state." David Robertson, Byrnes's astute biographer, has noted rightly that "rather than becoming Stimson's bellicose atomic diplomat intent upon intimidating the Soviet Union, Byrnes' diplomacy at his first postwar conference was based upon his willingness to offer the Soviets a quid pro quo of diplomatic recognition of the Soviet regimes in Asia, in Eastern Europe, and in the Balkans in exchange for Soviet cooperation in quickly finalizing the drafts of the preliminary peace treaties." Byrnes certainly arrived in the British capital intent on making tangible progress on a number of issues.[14]

The London CFM meeting opened on September 11, the first of six conferences over the next year and a half where the foreign ministers attempted to resolve a variety of issues in hopes of forging a postwar settlement. Whatever his optimistic hopes for cooperation, Byrnes and

---

[12] Hamby, *Man of the People*, p. 340.
[13] Truman's Radio Address, September 1, 1945, *Public Papers of the President: Harry S. Truman, 1945*, p. 257.
[14] See Robertson, *Sly and Able*, pp. 446–447. (Robertson quoted Byrnes.)

Ernest Bevin quickly clashed with the obstinacy of Foreign Minister Molotov, who appeared resolved to prevent serious negotiations. After initial procedural disagreements and a full day, September 13, during which the foreign ministers failed to even greet each other at the formal conference table, Byrnes approached Molotov at a reception at the House of Lords. In what Walter Brown, Byrnes's assistant, described as "typical Senatorial fashion," he asked when they might get "down to business." Indicative of what apparently held his attention, Molotov responded by asking Byrnes if he had "an atomic bomb in his side pocket." Byrnes, continuing in good senatorial form, told Molotov: "You don't know Southerners. We carry our artillery in our hip pocket." He went on in a good-natured fashion to tell Molotov that "if you don't cut out all this stalling and let us get down to work, I am going to pull an atomic bomb out of my hip pocket and let you have it."[15] His tone contained not the slightest hint of a serious threat. Molotov and his interpreter greeted the comments with laughter and so ended Byrnes's humorous yet most direct effort ever to raise his possession of the atomic bomb to his Soviet colleague. It could hardly have been done more benignly and amusingly even if deliberately planned, and it had all the impact of a feather landing on a cushion.[16]

Later in the meeting Molotov even came close to mocking Byrnes for the American atomic monopoly. On September 17 after Byrnes gave a speech at a formal dinner at St. James's Palace, Molotov offered a "tribute" to Byrnes in which he noted Byrnes's eloquence and then added sarcastically that Byrnes also had an atomic bomb.[17] In response to this provocation Byrnes kept his cool and worked to further genuine negotiations. One might ask however, why, after Molotov so quickly shattered his hopes that the atomic bomb's mere presence in the American arsenal would make the Soviets more amenable to negotiation, the secretary of state did not ratchet up the pressure. Pointing to the effective American atomic monopoly into the 1950s, John Lewis Gaddis framed a related if broader question – "so why did Washington not issue an ultimatum demanding the dismantlement of Soviet authority in eastern Europe, perhaps even of

---

[15] Brown Diary, September 13, 1945, Byrnes Papers, Folder 602.
[16] One can only endorse the conclusion of McGeorge Bundy that "revisionist historians have accused Byrnes of practicing atomic diplomacy in this [London] session, but the records do not bear them out." See Bundy, *Danger and Survival*, p. 145. For a recent example of exaggeration of Byrnes's "atomic diplomacy" at the London CFM see Campbell Craig and Sergey Radchenko, *The Atomic Bomb and the Origins of the Cold War* (New Haven, CT, 2008), p. 98.
[17] See the report in Brown Diary, September 17, 1945, Byrnes Papers, Folder 602. For more on Molotov and the atomic bomb see Holloway, *Stalin and the Bomb*, p. 156.

the Soviet dictatorship itself, backed up by the threat ... that Moscow would be bombed if it didn't go along?"[18] The reasons for the broad American reticence require extended discussion, but certainly it must be accepted that at the time of the London meeting Byrnes had no intention of trying to intimidate the Soviet Union into concessions. He simply didn't think in these categories. For him Japan had needed to be intimidated into surrender to stop the ghastly war and the loss of American lives, but the immediate postwar circumstance called for no threats of such horrendous measures. No ultimatums would be put before the Soviets. Whatever his frustrations in dealing with Molotov, Byrnes soldiered on in trying to reach substantive agreements to secure the postwar peace well into 1946 knowing that the American atomic monopoly brought him little, if any, diplomatic advantage.

Back in Washington Stimson took advantage of Byrnes's absence and presented his completed report directly to Truman at a meeting on September 12. They read it together and the president learned of the key recommendation that he approach the Soviets directly with a view to arranging for international control of the bomb.[19] Truman scheduled a full cabinet meeting to consider the question, and this was held on Stimson's very last day in office, September 21. The confusion and divisions within the Truman administration were well displayed at the session. Stimson made his case for outreach to the Soviets. Navy Secretary James Forrestal led those who resisted such an initiative because of their increasing concerns about the Soviet Union's international behavior and ambitions. Indicative that the Byrnes state department hardly worked from some coherent policy designed to utilize the atomic bomb in its diplomacy, Acting Secretary Acheson proved a strong supporter of Stimson rather than adopting the more restrictive stance favored by his absent departmental chief. Forrestal summarized in his diary that Acheson, the renowned cold warrior of the future, "saw no alternative except to give full information to the Russians, however for some quid pro quo in the way of a mutual exchange of information. [He] could not conceive of a world in which we were hoarders of military secrets from our Allies, particularly this great Ally upon our cooperation with whom rests the future peace of the world."[20]

---

[18] Gaddis, *Surprise, Security, and the American Experience*, p. 62. See also pp. 62–63 for Gaddis's discussion of the issue.

[19] For Stimson's memorandum of September 11, 1945, outlining his full position for Truman see Robert H. Ferrell, ed., *Harry S. Truman and the Bomb: A Documentary History* (Worland, WY, 1996), pp. 77–82.

[20] Millis, ed., *The Forrestal Diaries*, pp. 94–96.

Truman, influenced mostly by Stimson and Acheson, eventually agreed after the lengthy cabinet meeting and subsequent written submissions to pursue efforts to place atomic energy under international control so as to avoid a devastating arms race.[21] The hope that motivated this action rested in a desire to assure stable relations among the major powers in a situation where the American atomic monopoly could not be forever guaranteed.[22] It reflected a continued willingness to collaborate with the Soviet Union.

In London Byrnes acquiesced in the cabinet decision on international control of atomic energy whatever his hesitations in that regard. He maintained an admirable focus on working to reach settlements with an obtuse Molotov who gave no ground on the crucial issue of lessening Soviet domination of Balkan nations like Bulgaria and Rumania. Consistent with their compromise arrangement at Potsdam, Byrnes made clear to his Soviet counterpart that he understood the Soviet need for "friendly" governments in Eastern Europe. Nonetheless, he encouraged Molotov to permit some limited openness such as allowing American news correspondents into these countries. Such measures, he explained, would help facilitate the U.S. Senate's ratification of the treaties they might negotiate.[23] Molotov remained quite unmoved by Byrnes's entreaties. Revealing his strategy that offense constituted the best defense the Soviet minister attacked Byrnes's flanks with demands regarding Soviet participation in the occupation of Japan and demands for certain Italian colonies in Africa that only deepened Byrnes's fears about Soviet expansionism. The London Conference crawled to an inglorious end without substantial progress and with "Big Three unity in serious disarray."[24]

The disarray surprised and troubled Byrnes. He had ventured to London not to implement some atomic diplomacy strategy to force Soviet compliance, but to make progress on a postwar settlement through

---

[21] Stimson's efforts, the cabinet discussion, and Truman's subsequent decisions are well outlined in Bundy, *Danger and Survival*, pp. 136–145. Truman asked participants after the September 21 meeting to submit their views in writing to him. For the counsel of Dean Acheson, who warned in his cover memorandum that "a policy of secrecy is both futile and dangerous," see Acheson to Truman, September 25, 1945, Truman Papers, PSF, Box 199.

[22] For a good summary of the American international control efforts see Bundy, *Danger and Survival*, pp. 145–161.

[23] For Byrnes's discussions with Molotov see Bohlen minutes, Byrnes-Molotov Conversations, September 16 and 19, 1945, *FRUS 1945*, II, pp. 194–201, 243–247. Walter Brown suggests that Byrnes approached Molotov in a "pleading manner" appealing to him to "relax his position in the Balkans for the peace of the world." Brown diary entry, September 16, 1945, Byrnes Papers, Folder 602.

[24] Gaddis, *The United States and the Origins of the Cold War*, p. 266.

genuine compromise. In London, however, he worried about what Soviet obstinacy foreshadowed and he found Molotov almost impossible to deal with. Byrnes even told Walter Brown on September 21 that "M[olotov] was trying to do in a slick dip [?] way what Hitler had tried to do in domineering smaller countries by force." Yet Byrnes did not quickly give up hope on the possibilities of negotiation and shift to some strategy designed to confront an intransigent Soviet Union. He still sought cooperation. Ironically and almost laughably in light of Stalin's domination over and control of Molotov, Byrnes concluded that he would have to appeal over Molotov to Stalin. He thought "Stalin wants peace" and even expressed fear "for the world if Stalin should die."[25] He resolved to continue his efforts to negotiate agreements at another foreign ministers meeting, which he wanted held in Moscow, where he would have direct contact with Stalin.

On his return to Washington Byrnes put the best public face on a bad situation by informing a national radio audience of the "considerable areas of agreement" among the foreign ministers and that the London Conference demonstrated "the hard reality that none of us can expect to write the peace in our own way." He looked ahead to "a second and better chance to get on with the peace."[26] Byrnes's rather accommodating position must be well appreciated by all those who seek to relate the U.S. possession of the atomic bomb to the formulation of foreign policy. Furthermore, the temptation to view developments through the lens of the later Cold War conflict should be resisted. Perhaps surprisingly, in the months immediately after the London CFM meeting the atomic bombs played little direct role in shaping the policies that Byrnes fashioned for the Truman administration. In his report to the American people on the London meeting the secretary of state had confessed his belief "that peace and political progress in international affairs as in domestic affairs depend upon intelligent compromise" and he acted on that belief. While critical of the Soviet's procedural maneuvers at the London meeting, Byrnes "remained undeterred by temporary setbacks" and promised not to "relax in our efforts to achieve a just and lasting peace for ourselves and all nations."[27]

In making his plans both in London and for the future Byrnes faced no restraints from the president he served. As Robert Messer clarified,

---

[25] Brown Diary September 21, 1945, Byrnes Papers, Folder 602.
[26] Byrnes radio address, October 5, 1945, *Department of State Bulletin*, Vol. 13 (October 7, 1945), pp. 507–512.
[27] Byrnes address, October 5, 1945, *Dept of State Bulletin*, Vol. 13, pp. 507, 508, 510, 512.

Truman "gave no indication of any special interest in the details of Byrnes's negotiations" in London. He gave Byrnes "general support and encouragement" and allowed him considerable discretion in determining American tactics and strategy.[28] Truman's dependence on and trust in Byrnes remained very strong. After determining to proceed with plans for international control of atomic energy he made clear that his secretary of state would have the responsibility for supervising all discussions on the topic.[29] He deemed Byrnes as the key person to help him carry forth the plans to secure the postwar peace.

Truman's own thinking at this time is, to be kind, a little hard to pin down. It is frankly rather confusing and reflects his continued uncertainty and insecurity on foreign policy issues. Occasional statements suggested he hewed toward a tougher policy regarding the Soviet Union, but these were countered by reassurances of his continued hopes for accommodation with Stalin's Russia. Truman included both of these broad approaches in the Navy Day speech he gave on October 27. Seemingly unperturbed by the contradictions of the two approaches the president spoke of continued American military strength and promised an American foreign policy "based firmly on fundamental principles of righteousness and justice," and on refusing to "compromise with evil." The United States, he assured his listeners, would never recognize governments forced on their peoples. Despite such simplistic assertions Truman also affirmed the importance of collaboration with wartime allies. In words that he presumably meant to be heard in foreign capitals such as Moscow the president insisted that "the world cannot afford any letdown in the united determination of the allies in this war to accomplish a lasting peace." He stated that "the cooperative spirit of the allies" could not be allowed to disintegrate. In support of Byrnes's desire for compromise and negotiation he asserted that "there are no conflicts of interest among the victorious powers so deeply rooted that they cannot be resolved."[30]

Whatever their concerns about Soviet behavior neither Truman nor Byrnes had given up on the goal of securing a cooperative postwar relationship with the Soviet Union. They remained wedded to a Rooseveltian vision of collaborating with Moscow to secure postwar peace. To this end Truman placed special hopes in the successful working of the United Nations organization. Also, like Byrnes, he expressed a special confidence

---

[28] Messer, *The End of an Alliance*, p. 126.   [29] Bundy, *Danger and Survival*, p. 145.
[30] Truman speech, October 27, 1945, *Public Papers of the President: Harry S. Truman, 1945*, pp. 431–438.

in dealing with Stalin whom he deemed to be "a moderating influence in the present Russian government." Truman admitted in late October of 1945 that serious differences existed between the Soviets and the Americans, but he believed "that we could work them out amicably if we gave ourselves time."[31] He planned to offer such time to his secretary of state and to leave him to undertake the necessary work. The president had other matters to occupy him. Indicative of his overall thrust Truman wanted to take another part of the Rooseveltian legacy and to extend it and put his own stamp upon it. On September 6, 1945 he sent a message to the Congress defending central New Deal programs and calling for their enhancement and development. He included in his message the economic "bill of rights," which FDR earlier had outlined with its calls for decent employment, housing, health care, and education for all Americans. The message marked the real beginning of his "Fair Deal" in which he laid out "the details of the program of liberalism and progressivism," which he later presented as "the foundation of my administration."[32] Truman's deep commitment to full employment made clear that he would not retreat from the activist government that characterized FDR's administration. Over the coming weeks and months Truman forwarded legislation to the Congress to implement the goals outlined in his message including plans for a national health program and for an expansion of the Social Security system.

Among the various messages Truman sent to Congress in October, 1945 was a call for Congress to create new arrangements to oversee the Manhattan Project infrastructure and to provide guidance for the future development of atomic energy. He asked for legislation to create an Atomic Energy Commission to oversee this revolutionary new domain. In the final section of his message he also called for initial steps to implement international control of the powerful new discovery. Clearly more influenced by Stimson and Acheson than by Forrestal, he proposed initial talks with Great Britain and Canada and "then with other nations, in an effort to effect agreement on the conditions under which cooperation might replace rivalry in the field of Atomic power."[33] This broad outline guided the efforts of the Truman administration in the coming months. It further clarified that it was the question of control of atomic weapons

---

[31] Truman quoted in Gaddis, *The United States and the Origins of the Cold War*, p. 275.

[32] Truman, *Year of Decisions*, p. 532. For Truman's message, September 6, 1945, see *Public Papers of the President: Harry S. Truman, 1945*, pp. 263–309. For thoughtful analysis of the content and significance of this address see Hamby, *Man of the People*, pp. 362–364.

[33] Truman's Special Message to Congress on Atomic Energy, October 3, 1945, *Public Papers of the President: Harry S. Truman, 1945*, pp. 362–366; quotation from p. 366.

rather than their use as an instrument of diplomacy that dominated the thinking of the early Truman administration. Indeed, this remained the guiding stance for the United States well into the future. Far from dominating the diplomacy of the Truman administration during the months after the Pacific War ended, the atomic bombs and the means to control them emerged primarily as subjects for diplomacy.

CHAPTER 9

The Atomic Bomb and the Origins of the Cold War

The devastating atomic blows against Hiroshima and Nagasaki certainly helped end World War II, but did they simultaneously plant the seeds for future conflict among the victorious allies? Did the atomic blasts constitute in some way the opening shots in the Cold War struggle that dominated the postwar era? Could the Cold War have been avoided if Truman had refrained from using the atomic bomb against Japan? Some attention surely must be given these questions here, although the detailed story of how nuclear weapons contributed in the long contest between the United States and the Soviet Union lies beyond the scope of this study. Understanding the American approach regarding these weapons in the early Cold War casts a certain light back on Hiroshima and Nagasaki, and it puts their use into a broader perspective. It clarifies that the atomic bomb did not cause the Cold War but rather it helped shape how the Cold War developed. The issues of nuclear weapons control and competition became unavoidably intertwined with the developing Cold War confrontation between the Soviet Union and the United States. Yet, it must be emphasized, they reflected the conflict rather than serving to provoke it. Comprehending the essential and immediate cause of outbreak of the Cold War assures that one avoids any exaggeration of the place of nuclear weapons in precipitating the bitter struggle.

The American effort well into 1946 remained focused on international control of atomic weapons rather than on either their use as an instrument for diplomacy or their incorporation into American military strategy. Indecision and even confusion continued to characterize American foreign policy from late 1945 through late 1946. Only slowly and in a rather disorganized manner did the United States object to Soviet policies that it deemed threatening to its interests and world peace. Neither Truman nor Byrnes, it must be said, possessed a clear understanding of the nature of Stalin and his regime at the time. They wobbled and wavered in forming a coherent policy to respond to Soviet actions.[1]

The ad hoc and rather confused nature of the Truman administration's policy making revealed itself in early November of 1945 after the president announced he would meet Prime Minister Clement Attlee and the Canadian leader William MacKenzie King to discuss international control of atomic energy. When Vannevar Bush, the wartime director of the Office of Scientific Research and Development, approached Byrnes barely a week before the scheduled meeting of the leaders whose nations had cooperated to develop the atomic bomb, he learned that "there was no organization for the meeting, no agenda being prepared, and no American plan in form to present." So much for suggestions of atomic weapons somehow shaping postwar American strategy! Byrnes deftly took the chance to task a surprised Bush with formulating such a plan, which he quickly did and it formed the basis for the Anglo-American-Canadian agreement signed on November 15.[2] Here Truman endorsed an approach of cautious openness regarding the sharing of atomic technology that had its antecedents in Stimson's advice. The policy neither rushed to engage the Soviets nor did it signal any desire to exclude them. The declaration observed that no single nation could maintain a monopoly on atomic weapons and in rather high-minded fashion it called both for using atomic energy to benefit all mankind and for the prevention of its use for "destructive purposes." To these ends the signatories declared their willingness to allow for the exchange of basic scientific information. Such exchanges would be overseen by a specially created UN commission that also would work to control the use of atomic energy for peaceful purposes only, and would arrange eventually for the elimination of atomic weapons from national armaments. The commission also would bear responsibility for instituting a system of inspections and compliance procedures to effectively safeguard the application of atomic technology to peaceful ends. The work of the commission, they concluded, "should proceed by separate stages, the successful

---

[1] I deal with this subject in detail in my *From Roosevelt to Truman: Potsdam, Hiroshima, and the Cold War* (New York, 2007), pp. 262–306. For other views that accord greater significance to the atomic bombs in the outbreak of the Cold War see Campbell Craig and Sergey Radchenko, *The Atomic Bomb and the Origins of the Cold War* (New Haven, CT, 2008); and Michael Gordin, *Red Cloud at Dawn.*

[2] For the direct quotation and more elaborate discussion of this subject see Gaddis, *The United States and the Origins of the Cold War*, pp. 270–271.

completion of one of which will develop the necessary confidence of the world before the next stage is undertaken."[3]

The consignment of this challenging issue to the fledgling United Nations no doubt pleased Truman who placed great hopes in that body. Secretary Byrnes, thinking more directly in terms of major power relations, saw that the matter of the proposed commission should be discussed with the Soviets before the first meeting of the UN General Assembly scheduled for January in London.[4] This issue provided him with a further motivation to pursue a meeting of Soviet, British, and American foreign ministers in Moscow in December, which he proposed on November 23.[5] Byrnes gained Ernest Bevin's grudging agreement to participate and soon set off. Prompted by the Truman-Attlee-King declaration's call to fashion a UN commission to oversee atomic energy matters, Byrnes placed this matter high on his proposed agenda. He adopted a plan aimed at facilitating negotiations that emphasized the exchange of scientific information, and he even implied that such exchanges might be authorized before the safeguards called for in the tripartite declaration were in place.

In Moscow, Byrnes made progress in his search for agreements on a range of important matters including peace treaties with the Balkan nations and occupation arrangements in Japan, Korea, and Manchuria. The American diplomat rather pragmatically accepted that Europe had been divided and he aimed to make the best of it. He hoped that a cooperative relationship might be maintained with the Soviets, and to that end he tried to limit the issues over which they might conflict.[6] Importantly, Byrnes gained Molotov's commitment to cosponsor a resolution at the initial session of the General Assembly of the UN, which would establish a commission for the international control of atomic energy. The prospects for some cooperation on this matter still appeared quite promising.

The achievements of the Moscow conference pleased Byrnes, who thought the meeting laid the groundwork for further constructive negotiations at the upcoming first session of the UN General Assembly.[7] His hopes

---

[3] For the formal statement see President's News Conference, November 15, 1945, *Public Papers of the President: Harry S. Truman, 1945*, pp. 472–475.

[4] Gaddis, *The United States and the Origins of the Cold War*, pp. 276–277.

[5] Byrnes to Molotov included in Byrnes to Harriman, November 23, 1945, *FRUS 1945*, Vol. II, p. 578.

[6] I am greatly influenced in my analysis here by the insightful work of Marc Trachtenberg in his *A Constructed Peace*, pp. 14–15.

[7] Robertson even suggests that Byrnes was "ebullient" because he believed that "he had 'gotten through' to Stalin and that he had successfully continued the Soviet-U.S. entente cordiale into the postwar world." See his *Sly and Able*, p. 452.

and attitude, however, contrasted markedly with those of his British counterpart, who found the Soviet military intrusion into the heart of Europe along with the apparent plan to totally dominate the Eastern half of the continent much more troubling. Ernest Bevin looked beyond the comity of the Moscow meeting to the broad geopolitical realities and favored a more forceful approach to the Soviets than did Byrnes. An appreciation of their differing outlooks aids in understanding the causes and outbreak of the Cold War. Bevin, the former trade unionist and committed social democrat, felt no need to conciliate or accommodate the Soviet Union. He wanted decent relations with Moscow, but evident Soviet expansionist tendencies worried him greatly. In an off-the-record conversation with British diplomatic correspondents on January 1, 1946, he explained that Russia was "seeking to put around herself for security purposes whole groups of satellites in the south, east and west with the view of controlling every kind of place which is likely to come in contact with her."[8] It was not only the increasing communist domination in Eastern Europe that bothered him but also the rising appeal of communist parties in France and Italy and, even more importantly, the threat of further Soviet expansion in the Mediterranean and the Middle East.

Bevin recognized that Soviet expansion represented a major threat to traditional British interests. While Truman and Byrnes – still in Rooseveltian mold – worked to settle issues with the Soviets, the rather coarse British foreign minister courageously raised objections and sought to contest threatening Soviet behavior. The Soviets clearly appreciated this reality. Britain became the principal target of Soviet propaganda in late 1945 and 1946, as British and European scholars have pointed out.[9] In fact, the Norwegian scholar Geir Lundestad argued correctly that "in 1945–46 the main antagonists were Britain and the Soviet Union, not the United States and the Soviet Union."[10] Although it is not always well appreciated by American historians who prefer to write the history of the Cold War as simply a bipolar confrontation, the British so objected to Soviet behavior that it is right to speak of the "Anglo-Soviet Cold War."[11]

[8] Bevin, quoted in Alan Bullock, *Ernest Bevin: Foreign Secretary, 1945–1951* (New York, 1983), p. 214.

[9] See especially Bullock, *Ernest Bevin, Foreign Secretary*, pp. 216–217.

[10] Geir Lundestad, *The United States and Western Europe since 1945: From "Empire" by Invitation to Transatlantic Drift* (New York, 2003), p. 48.

[11] See Fraser Harbutt's chapter entitled "Anglo-Soviet Cold War, United States–Soviet Rapprochement," in his *The Iron Curtain: Churchill, America, and the Origins of the Cold War* (New York, 1986), pp. 117–150.

Issues concerning the atomic bomb obviously played no role whatsoever in this incipient struggle. Soviet actions and ambitions were what troubled Bevin, and he pursued his good fight through 1946 hoping for American support, although never sure of what the American response would be.

Bevin's effort got notable assistance from the alarms raised about Soviet expansion and intentions by George Kennan in his influential Long Telegram and by Winston Churchill in his famous Iron Curtain address. Writing from Moscow and acting as ambassador at the U.S. embassy, Kennan explained in February, 1946 that Soviet power was "neither schematic nor adventuristic. It does not work by fixed plans. It does not take unnecessary risks. Impervious to the logic of reason, it is highly sensitive to the logic of force." He asserted that Soviet power usually withdrew upon strong resistance and, he emphasized, "if the adversary has sufficient force and makes clear his readiness to use it, he rarely has to do so."[12] Kennan's cable contributed to the construction of the intellectual supports for a developing disposition of firmness toward the Soviet Union, and at the same time it tore at the heart of Roosevelt's notion that a reassured and "domesticated" Soviet Union might be integrated into a new world system. It also raised doubts about whether the Byrnes approach based on bargaining and compromise could truly facilitate a stable settlement with the USSR. Stalin, Kennan rightly judged, proved a figure beyond reassurance. Thus, as John Lewis Gaddis encapsulated the Kennan argument, "there could be ... no permanent resolution of differences with such a government, which relied on the fiction of external threat to maintain internal legitimacy."[13]

In his famous speech given at Westminster College in Fulton, Missouri in March, 1946, with the American president beside him on the dais, former Prime Minister Churchill publicly expressed similar concerns to Kennan's private communication. The British statesman observed that no one knew "what Soviet Russia and its Communist international organization intends to do in the immediate future, or what are the limits, if any, to their expansive and proselytizing tendencies." Professing his admiration for the Russian people and for Stalin and his understanding of legitimate Russian security needs, he nevertheless felt obliged to place before his audience "certain facts about the present position in Europe." There

---

[12] For the Long Telegram see Kennan to Secretary of State, February 22, 1946, *FRUS 1946*, VI, pp. 696–709.

[13] John Lewis Gaddis, *Strategies of Containment: A Critical Appraisal of Postwar American National Security Policy* (New York, 1982), p. 20.

followed his famous *and* accurate assessment: "From Stettin in the Baltic to Trieste in the Adriatic, an iron curtain has descended across the Continent. Behind that line lie all the capitals of the ancient states of Central and Eastern Europe. Warsaw, Berlin, Prague, Vienna, Budapest, Belgrade, Bucharest, and Sofia, all these famous cities and the populations around them lie in what I must call the Soviet sphere, and all are subject in one form or another, not only to Soviet influence but to a very high and, in many cases, increasing measure of control from Moscow." Turning to Soviet intentions Churchill discerned, again with telling accuracy, that the Soviets did not desire war. Rather, "what they desire is the fruits of war and indefinite expansion of their power and doctrines." In light of this and his belief that the Soviets respected strength rather than weakness, Churchill argued that an Anglo-American association must reach "a good understanding on all points with Russia under the general authority of the United Nations Organization."[14]

The combination of the Kennan and Churchill efforts certainly helped both to erode the legitimacy of the established policy of cooperation with the Soviet Union, and to transform the perception of the Soviets in the American official mind from difficult ally to potential foe. But it is striking to gauge how little positive impact on policy this new perception of the Soviets actually exercised. The United States possessed by the end of March 1946 an enhanced disposition to challenge and to confront the Soviets on particular incidents. Byrnes himself certainly displayed this in standing up vigorously and forcing the Soviets to abandon their military occupation of northern Iran that very month.[15] But such a disposition hardly constituted a coherent policy that could be explained to the American Congress and people. The Long Telegram and the "iron curtain" address in no sense put an end to the floundering in American policy formulation.

Confirmation that the combined Kennan/Churchill salvo failed to provoke a major reversal in American policy came with the determination of policy on the international control of atomic weapons. Byrnes tasked Acheson to lead the formulation of an American proposal to submit to the newly established UN atomic energy commission, and Acheson thereupon built upon his earlier efforts supporting Stimson. With the assistance

---

[14] Churchill's speeches from his U.S. visit in 1946 including the "iron curtain" speech entitled "The Sinews of Peace," March 5, 1946, are included in Churchill Papers, Churchill Archives Center, Cambridge, England, Churchill Series 5/4.
[15] For a full account of Byrnes's efforts on Iran see Robertson, *Sly and Able*, pp. 462–476.

of David Lilienthal, chairman of the Tennessee Valley Authority, and Robert Oppenheimer, he fashioned the "Acheson-Lilienthal report." This document's proposals called for genuine international control of nuclear research and technology. Made public on March 28, 1946, the report argued that the only way to preclude the use of nuclear energy for weapons purposes was to create an international authority that would exercise a monopoly over nuclear research and development. It proposed a supranational International Atomic Development Authority that would be entrusted with all phases of the development and use of atomic energy. It would have the power to manage, control, and license all related activities, but would not have specific powers to apply sanctions against wrongdoers. Also, as Robert Beisner explained, "precisely to attract Soviet support, they [Acheson, Lilienthal, and Oppenheimer] deemphasized inspections, which they saw as resistant to accomplishment, incapable of offering foolproof protection, and profoundly intrusive to Russian leaders."[16]

When Truman and Byrnes, in a bid to assure congressional support for the American initiative, appointed Bernard Baruch, an elderly, vain but politically well-connected financier, as a special envoy to present the American proposal at the United Nations they indicated no dissatisfaction with the Acheson-Lilienthal proposal.[17] But Baruch took the initiative and revised the plan to include tougher inspections, sanctions for violations, and a specific ban on using the UN Security Council veto to escape punishment in this area.[18] In April, 1946, Baruch had pressed Oppenheimer on the fundamental point of whether the Acheson-Lilienthal plan was "compatible with the current Soviet system of government." In reply, the brilliant physicist admitted some concerns in that regard, but argued that the American position "should be to make an

---

[16] Beisner, "Patterns of Peril: Dean Acheson Joins the Cold Warriors, 1945–1946," *Diplomatic History*, Vol. 20 (Summer, 1996), p. 330. For Oppenheimer's important role in drafting the plan see Bird and Sherwin, *American Prometheus*, pp. 340–342.

[17] On the reasons for Baruch's appointment see Truman, *Memoirs*, Vol. II, *Years of Trial and Hope* (New York, 1956), pp. 20–21. On this appointment also see Byrnes's letter to Baruch of April 19, 1946, in which the secretary of state explained that "I have advised you that I am favorably impressed by the report which has come to be called the State Department report and which was prepared under the direction of Mr. Acheson. I have, however, advised you that I am not of the opinion that it is the last word on the subject and, on the contrary, that I shall give careful consideration to any views that may be presented by you after you consider the problem." Byrnes to Baruch, April 19, 1946, Truman Papers, PSF, Box 113.

[18] On Baruch and his nuclear activities see Margaret Coit, *Mr. Baruch* (Boston, 1957), pp. 565–585. Also see Hewlett and Anderson, *The New World*, pp. 562–576.

honorable proposal and thus find out whether they [Soviets] have the will to cooperate."[19] Acheson and Lilienthal certainly endorsed this approach to obtain Soviet cooperation through to the middle of the year. Baruch, however, proved unwilling to forego inspections and sanctions. He forced a showdown in June that compelled Truman, who appeared to decide more in sorrow than in anger, to endorse his delegate to the UN. He could hardly afford Baruch's resignation, which assuredly would have prompted a congressional outcry regarding security concerns. Furthermore, by July the president increasingly sympathized with Baruch's position. He confirmed that "we should not under any circumstances throw away our gun until we are sure the rest of the world can't arm against us."[20] He didn't rule out international control, but any arrangements could not gamble with American security by simply relying on Russian good faith. In retrospect, this seems a reasonable position especially given the nature of the Soviet system and the sustained campaign of Soviet espionage to gain information of the atomic bomb. That it took Truman until mid-1946 to reach it, and then only because Baruch brought matters to a head, is truly notable.

Baruch unveiled the American plan to beat its nuclear sword into a ploughshare at the United Nations on June 14. It included the cautionary provisions for inspections and sanctions. To absolutely no one's surprise, the Soviet Union rejected the American proposal, quickly dubbed the Baruch Plan, outright, and, despite months of further discussion, no agreement was ever reached. The Soviet representative, Andrei Gromyko, offered a counterproposal that called simply for the prohibition of the production and use of nuclear weapons, and for the destruction of existing stockpiles. He offered no serious inspection system to monitor compliance.[21] The Soviet motives in rejecting the American scheme obviously lay in fear that the Baruch Plan would subject the Soviet economy and scientific community to control by a body that would be controlled by Western governments. Presumably it would reveal the extent of Soviet progress to secure their own atomic weapons. At a broader level, any effective inspection system would seriously breach the Iron Curtain. This Stalin refused to permit. To understand why one must grasp well the Soviet dictator's ambitions after World War II.

[19] Oppenheimer quote in Bird and Sherwin, *American Prometheus*, p. 343.
[20] Truman to Baruch, July 10, 1946, quoted in Truman, *Years of Trial and Hope*, p. 25.
[21] For excellent brief summaries of the Baruch and Gromyko plans see Joseph M. Siracusa, *Nuclear Weapons: A Very Short Introduction* (Oxford, 2008), pp. 30–36.

While judging the extent of Stalin's expansionist intentions and the nature of the Soviet threat has proved to be a controversial topic among western historians, the end of the Cold War and the limited opening of Soviet and East European archives have allowed historians to shed light on Stalin's motives and actions. While some emphasized that Stalin, although obsessed by an "insatiable craving" for security, possessed no master plan for expansion and acted opportunistically, it has become difficult to ignore the Soviet dictator's unappeasable appetite for control.[22] This was a man, after all, who feared and distrusted his very own people who had expended twenty million lives to defend their homeland. Thousands upon thousands of Soviet war veterans were dispatched at war's end to the Gulag Archipelago in a vain effort to reassure a twisted and vile leader.

In retrospect it can be seen that Stalin – at least theoretically – faced two broad choices at the war's end. The first, as articulated by Vladimir A. Pozniakov, involved "political and economic cooperation with the Allies and with the west in general." Such an approach "could lessen tensions that had surfaced in interallied relations by the end of the war, lower the level of military expenditures, and thus allow more rapid restoration of the Soviet national economy and higher living standards in the Soviet Union." The second possibility "was to impose tighter control over the Soviet people, crushing hopes for change in the Soviet political and social system" so as to provide the basis for forging a vast Soviet empire, supposedly needed to guarantee Soviet security.[23] Stalin, of course, chose the latter direction, and so planned for a policy of confrontation with the West. The American possession of an atomic bomb, it appears, proved quite irrelevant to either forming or even to moderating his ultimate ambitions.

Ironically, Stalin might have been able to pursue his chosen approach of sovietization of a vast territory without much objection from the United States, if he had been able to limit his external goals to an East European sphere of influence. If he had learned a lesson from the Iran episode in

---

[22] See for example Vojtech Mastney, *The Cold War and Soviet Insecurity: The Stalin Years* (New York, 1996); and Vladislav Zubok and Constantine Pleshakov, *Inside the Kremlin's Cold War: From Stalin to Khrushchev* (Cambridge, MA, 1996). See the critical review of these works in Richard C. Raack, "The Cold War Revisionists Kayoed: New Books Dispel More Historical Darkness," *World Affairs*, Vol. 162 (Fall, 1999), pp. 43–62. Also see Ilya Gaiduk, "Stalin: Three Approaches to One Phenomenon," *Diplomatic History*, Vol. 23 (Winter, 1999), pp. 119–125.

[23] Vladimir V. Pozniakov, "Commoners, Commissars, and Spies: Soviet Policies and Society 1945," in Arnold A. Offner and Theodore A. Wilson, eds., *Victory in Europe 1945: From World War to Cold War* (Lawrence, KS, 2000), p. 197.

March of 1946 and sat back contentedly to enjoy an empire that reached beyond the accomplishment of any of his Czarist forebears, then the Cold War might have been averted. But he could not. Stalin overreached and moved far beyond cementing his control of Eastern Europe so as to threaten both in the Mediterranean, particularly in Turkey, and also in Western Europe. In this disastrous choice lies the immediate origins of the Cold War. Fundamental differences over ideology, political, and economic systems, and ways of life assuredly underlay the conflict, but it was Stalin's paranoid definition of security that effectively provoked the United States to act, and to do what Ernest Bevin had long requested. Turkey and Germany provided the occasions for the initial, major American actions to counter Soviet pressures. From late 1946 and then especially in 1947 the Americans moved to replace the British as the essential counterforce to Soviet expansion and the Cold War was on in earnest. With the Truman Doctrine and the Marshall Plan the Truman administration began its sustained effort to contain Soviet expansion.

The inability to agree on the means to control atomic energy must be viewed then as a symptom of the suspicion and mistrust engendered by the Cold War rather than as a cause of the developing conflict. Lamentations over the failure to secure a regime of international control over atomic weapons should not disguise this. The American possession of the atomic bombs hardly altered Stalin's attitudes or intentions – the Soviet leader did not frighten easily. At best, it might have made him more cautious in pursuit of his goals. As for the Americans, their nuclear monopoly hardly defined how they responded to the Soviets in the Cold War. The United States did proceed forward with a nuclear development and testing program, and in mid-1946 (with Soviet observers present) exploded two atomic bombs over Bikini Atoll in the western Pacific's Marshall Islands. But what is more striking in retrospect is the failure of the Truman administration to effectively incorporate the atomic bombs into its diplomatic and military strategy during the Cold War.[24] Truman signed the McMahon Act into law in 1946, and thereby placed a civilian agency, the Atomic Energy Commission (AEC), in charge of atomic weapons. The military were thereafter kept at arms length from them, although there was not really much to keep from anyone's reach up through 1948. Indicative of a lack of concern for applying atomic weapons in any coherent political-military strategy the Truman administration allowed the nuclear arsenal to

---

[24] This point is developed in David G. Coleman and Joseph M. Siracusa, *Real-World Nuclear Deterrence: The Making of International Strategy* (Westport, CT, 2006), pp. 5–9.

deteriorate in numbers and readiness, despite the 1946 test program. The distinguished Truman biographer Robert Ferrell concluded that "at the outset of 1947 there might have been, after assembly, a single bomb."[25] The administration's guiding assumption appeared to be that its mere possession of the atomic bomb would persuade the Soviets against breaching the peace for fear of precipitating an all-out war in which atomic bombs would be deployed. In the American mind the weapons worked largely to deter aggression by the vastly superior Soviet conventional forces. Such deterrence served as both a component of and complement to the developing strategy of containment.

Even during specific crisis situations Truman refrained from employing nuclear weapons as a means to intimidate or counter the Soviets and their allies. During the Berlin blockade crisis of 1948 Truman deployed B-29 bombers of the Strategic Air Command (SAC) to Europe, but the planes were not equipped for atomic payloads. The airlift of supplies into the besieged city emerged as the central element of his response to this blatant Soviet provocation rather than any atomic intimidation. Even during the Korean War when American forces faced a military disaster at the hands of masses of Chinese troops during the winter of 1950–1951, Truman refused to pursue the atomic option despite the entreaties of his theater commander, General Douglas MacArthur. In effect, Truman established a lasting pattern that nuclear weapons could deter conflict among major powers but they could not be utilized in limited warfare.

This pattern was etched deeper following the Soviet Union's detonation of an atomic bomb at Semipalatinsk, a site in northern Kazakhstan, on August 29, 1949, a date incidentally well before the CIA's estimate that predicted Soviet success in 1953. The startling discovery by the U.S. surveillance system shattered the implicit sense of security that the American atomic monopoly had engendered among U.S. policy makers.[26] In the years up to 1949, the United States had not met the Soviet challenge by initiating a major rearmament effort to obtain a conventional force capability to counter possible Soviet aggression in Europe or elsewhere. Far from implementing such a measure, Truman successfully limited defense spending for reasons of political popularity and fiscal responsibility. The atomic monopoly served as an effective deterrent, so policy makers hoped, against Soviet utilization of their larger conventional

---

[25] Robert H. Ferrell, *Harry S. Truman and the Cold War Revisionists* (Columbia, MO, 2006), pp. 50–51.

[26] See Bundy, *Danger and Survival*, pp. 197–231.

forces. But news that the Soviets now possessed the atomic bomb caused deep disquiet.

In response to the successful Soviet atomic test, President Truman authorized development of a thermonuclear weapon – the hydrogen bomb – after an emotional debate within his administration. The fierce argument divided AEC Chair Lilienthal from his fellow commission member Lewis Strauss, and it severed Robert Oppenheimer from fellow scientists and hydrogen bomb proponents like Ernest Lawrence and Edward Teller. It also led to a rupture within the State Department as strategists George Kennan and Paul Nitze squared off over the issue. In the end, Dean Acheson, the early proponent of international control who now served as secretary of state, decided against his friends Lilienthal and Oppenheimer, and guided Truman to proceed to develop the hydrogen bomb. McGeorge Bundy observed that this Truman decision ranks "second in importance only to Franklin Roosevelt's commitment of October 1941 [to build the atomic bomb]; it led straight on, with no second thought by the president, to the world's first full-scale thermonuclear explosion, on November 1, 1952. For the human race there was no turning back. The first Soviet device was tested less than a year later."[27] Despite its hefty ramifications, Truman found it not a difficult decision at all. A few days after making it, Truman, the plain-speaking Missourian, told a White House staff session "that we had got to do it – make the bomb – though no one wants to use it. But ... we have got to have it if only for bargaining purposes with the Russians."[28] This dynamic of fear and caution regarding the actual and potential capabilities of the opposing superpower fueled the subsequent arms race.

The horrendous costs of the arms race over the following four decades lends the quality of pathos to the courageous endeavors of men like Lilienthal, Oppenheimer, and Kennan to limit the development of nuclear weapons. Their efforts to foster international control arrangements certainly can seem to place them on the side of the angels while leaving the hydrogen bomb's proponents like Strauss, Teller, and Nitze among the seeming villains of the story. Yet the testimony of the great Soviet physicist Andrei Sakharov reveals that caution is warranted in brandishing such designations. Soviet work on a thermonuclear bomb had already begun in 1948 when a theoretical group (that included Sakharov) was established under the leadership of Igor Tamm. And as Sakharov clarified, Stalin fully

---

[27] Bundy, *Danger and Survival*, p. 197.
[28] Eben Ayers Diary, February 4, 1950, Eben A. Ayers Papers, HSTL, Box 17.

understood the potential of the new weapon and planned to develop and deploy it.[29] Any American offer of either a moratorium on research or proposals for verifiable arrangements were destined to fail. In such circumstances Truman's decision, albeit tragically, takes on a certain wisdom. The long nuclear arms race and its guiding strategy of mutually assured destruction surely warrants criticism of all sorts, except that no viable and secure alternative easily presented itself to take the place of the nuclear standoff. Gerald DeGroot has observed of "the Bomb" that "however amoral, expensive and seemingly bankrupt the policy, deterrence remains the most effective defense against nuclear weapons yet conceived."[30] One trusts it will retain its effectiveness in the future until a superior course emerges.

So it is that for over sixty-five years Hiroshima and Nagasaki remained the only instances in which nuclear weapons were used in warfare. The long period since their use in World War II came to be seen as a period of "nuclear peace" where there has been no major conflict between any nuclear states. The prospect of a conflict escalating to a nuclear holocaust proved an effective brake. The costs of war seemed simply unacceptable to rational statesmen. The atomic bomb had been developed to help end a war, and that it had done, but it also played a somewhat unforeseen role in preserving the long peace among the major powers that followed it. In his final major speech to the House of Commons on March 1, 1955, Winston Churchill called this "the process of sublime irony" in which nations of the world "reached a stage in [their] story where safety will be the sturdy child of terror, and survival the twin brother of annihilation."[31] Oppenheimer described this reality even more dramatically through his famous analogy of the American and Soviet superpowers as "two scorpions in a bottle, each capable of killing the other, but only at the risk of his own life."[32] Fortunately, that risk has never been run. One might speculate that the searing of Hiroshima and Nagasaki into the world's consciousness helped assure that.

Determining the real impact of nuclear weapons after World War II remains a subject where serious observers can differ.[33] There is much less

[29] Andrei Sakharov, *Memoirs*, trans. Richard Lourie (New York, 1990), pp. 98–100. Also see David Holloway, *The Soviet union and the Arms Race* (New Haven, CT, 1983), pp. 23–25.

[30] DeGroot, *The Bomb: A Life*, p. 351.

[31] Churchill speech, House of Commons, March 1, 1955, quoted in Martin Gilbert, *Churchill: A Life* (New York, 1991), p. 936.

[32] J. Robert Oppenheimer, "Atomic Weapons and American Policy," *Foreign Affairs* Vol. 31, No. 4 (July, 1953), p. 529.

[33] For a recent study that argues, although not convincingly, that nuclear weapons didn't matter much at all see John Mueller, *Atomic Obsession: Nuclear Alarmism from Hiroshima to Al-Qaeda* (Oxford, 2010).

room for speculation and debate regarding their use against Japan. Despite the continuing swirl of controversy that surrounds Harry Truman's decision to authorize the atomic bombings of two Japanese cities, some essential conclusions must be acknowledged. First, the principal motive for utilizing the new weapon lay in a potent mix of desire to force Japan's surrender and save American lives. Second, the atomic bombs contributed decisively in forcing that eventual surrender and in bringing the brutal war to an end prior to any costly invasion of the Japanese home islands. Furthermore, while the atomic bomb was never entirely separated from considerations of postwar international politics, the decision to use the weapon was not driven by these concerns. The atomic bombs were used primarily for a military purpose, and they proved effective in inflicting defeat on the Japanese. Truman and his associates did not seek "alternatives" to using the atomic bombs, but viable options that might have proved successful cannot be identified with any certainty – even in retrospect and when far removed from the pressures Truman was under in 1945. There was not an easily available and appropriate option that would have met the serious political and moral objections of the many later critics of Truman's decision. Therein lies the tragic dimension of the decision to use the atomic bombs to defeat Japan.

Suggested Readings

Those who want a comprehensive introduction to the variety of isses regarding the atomic bomb must consult Michael Kort's excellent *The Columbia Guide to Hiroshima and the Bomb* (New York: Columbia University Press, 2007). His insightful chapter on "Key Questions and Interpretations" is very helpful, and the book also contains a valuable collection of source documents. For the latter also see Dennis Merrill, *Documentary History of the Truman Presidency,* Vol. 1, *The Decision to Drop the Atomic Bomb on Japan* (Bethesda, MD: University Publications of America, 1995). For a helpful introduction to the development of nuclear weapons consult Joseph M. Siracusa, *Nuclear Weapons: A Very Short Introduction* (Oxford and New York: Oxford University Press, 2008). For detailed accounts of the development of the atomic bomb see Richard Rhodes, *The Making of the Atomic Bomb* (New York: Simon and Schuster, 1986); and Richard G. Hewlett and Oscar E. Anderson, Jr., *The New World, 1939–1946,* Vol. I, *A History of the United States Atomic Energy Commission* (University Park: Pennsylvania State University Press, 1962). Also important are Henry DeWolf Smyth, *Atomic Energy for Military Purposes: The Official Report on the Development of the Atomic Bomb under the Auspices of the United States Government, 1940–45* (Princeton, NJ: Princeton University Press, 1945); and Vincent C. Jones, *Manhattan: The Army and the Atomic Bomb* (Washington, D.C.: U.S. Government Printing Office, 1985). Mark Fiege evokes the experience at Los Alamos in his "The Atomic Scientists, the Sense of Wonder, and the Bomb," *Environmental History,* Vol. 12 (July, 2007), pp. 578–613.

On the British atomic contribution see Margaret Gowing, *Britain and Atomic Energy, 1939–1945* (New York: St. Martin's Press, 1964). David Holloway's *Stalin and the Bomb: The Soviet Union and Atomic Energy, 1939–1956* (New Haven, CT: Yale University Press, 1994), tells the story of the Soviet nuclear project. For details of Soviet espionage of the Manhattan Project see Allen Weinstein and Alexander Vassiliev, *The Haunted Wood: Soviet Espionage in America – the Stalin Era* (New York: Random House, 1999); and John Earl Haynes and Harvey Klehr, *Early Cold War Spies: The Espionage Trials That Shaped American Politics* (Cambridge and New York: Cambridge University Press, 2006).

The use of the atomic bombs has been the subject of intense debate among historians. This debate is reviewed in J. Samuel Walker, "The Decision to Use the Bomb: A Historiographical Update," in Michael J. Hogan, ed., *America in the World: The Historiography of American Foreign Relations Since 1941* (Cambridge and New York: Cambridge University Press, 1995), pp. 207–219. Walker updated his work ten years later in an essay where he discerned a "balanced position" emerging on Truman's use of the bomb. See his "Recent Literature on Truman's Atomic Bomb Decision: A Search for Middle Ground," *Diplomatic History*, Vol. 29 (April, 2005), pp. 311–334. For the most recent survey of the literature see Michael Kort, "The Historiography of Hiroshima: The Rise and Fall of Revisionism," *The New England Journal of History*, Vol. 64 (Fall, 2007), pp. 31–48.

The former Secretary of War Henry L. Stimson offered one of the earliest and most persuasive defenses of the use of atomic weapons in "The Decision to Use the Atomic Bomb," *Harper's Magazine*, Vol. 194 (February, 1947), pp. 97–107. This "orthodox" position was presented in detail and very cogently by Herbert Feis in two books that still warrant careful reading – *Japan Subdued: The Atomic Bomb and the End of the War in the Pacific* (Princeton, NJ: Princeton University Press, 1961); and *The Atomic Bomb and the End of World War II* (Princeton, NJ: Princeton University Press, 1966). For an early expression of the so-called revisionist case that argued that the atomic bomb was not necessary to secure the Japanese surrender, and that it was used to influence the Soviet Union see P. M. S. Blackett's *Fear, War, and the Bomb: Military and Political Consequences of Atomic Energy* (New York: McGraw Hill, 1949). This "atomic diplomacy" thesis received its most influential expression in Gar Alperovitz, *Atomic Diplomacy: Hiroshima and Potsdam* (New York: Vintage, 1965). Robert James Maddox courageously detailed the shoddy scholarship, which undergirded Alperovitz's work in *The New Left and the Origins of the Cold War* (Princeton, NJ: Princeton University Press, 1973).

The debate over the atomic bomb reached especially high temperatures around the fiftieth anniversary of use of the weapons against Hiroshima and Nagasaki. Works that promoted the revisionist case included Gar Alperovitz et al., *The Decision to Use the Atomic Bomb and the Architecture of an American Myth* (New York: Knopf, 1995); and Robert Jay Lifton and Greg Mitchell, *Hiroshima in America: Fifty Years of Denial* (New York: Putnam's Sons, 1995). Robert James Maddox, *Weapons for Victory: The Hiroshima Decision Fifty Years Later* (Columbia: University of Missouri Press, 1995), and Robert P. Newman, *Truman and the Hiroshima Cult* (East Lansing: Michigan State University Press, 1995) strongly defended Truman's decision.

Martin Sherwin and Barton Bernstein rejected the "atomic diplomacy" thesis, but still proved sympathetic to aspects of the revisionist argument. See Martin J. Sherwin, *A World Destroyed: The Atomic Bomb and the Grand Alliance* (New York: Vintage, 1975). Barton Bernstein's many important articles include "Roosevelt, Truman, and the Atomic Bomb, 1941–1945: A Reinterpretation," *Political Science Quarterly*, Vol. 90 (Spring, 1975), pp. 23–69; and "Understanding the Atomic Bomb and the Japanese Surrender: Missed Opportunities, Little-Known Near Disasters, and Modern Memory," *Diplomatic History*, Vol. 19 (Spring, 1995), pp. 227–273. J. Samuel Walker's *Prompt and Utter Destruction: Truman and the Use of Atomic Bombs* (Chapel Hill: University of North Carolina Press, 2007) is a helpful overview that struggles to provide a "balanced" interpretation.

The literature on the Pacific War and the end of World War II is extensive. For a masterful overview of the whole enormous conflict consult Gerhard L. Weinberg, *A World At Arms: A Global History of World War II* (New York: Cambridge University Press, 1994). Richard B. Frank's magisterial *Downfall: The End of the Imperial Japanese Empire* (New York: Random House, 1999) is the crucial work on this topic and must be engaged by all serious students of the subject. Edward J. Drea's books are also indispensable for appreciating the latter stages of the Pacific War. See his *MacArthur's ULTRA: Codebreaking and the War Against Japan, 1942–1945* (Lawrence: University of Kansas Press, 1992); and *In the Service of the Emperor: Essays on the Imperial Japanese Army* (Lincoln: University of Nebraska Press, 1998). On the ferocity of the Pacific War see Werner Gruhl, *Imperial Japan's World War Two, 1931–1945* (New Brunswick, NJ: Transaction Publishers, 2007); and John W. Dower, *War Without Mercy: Race and Power in the Pacific War* (New York: Pantheon Books, 1986), which emphasizes the dastardly impact of racial stereotypes in the Pacific conflict. On the final stages of the brutal conflict also see Max Hastings, *Retribution: The Battle for Japan, 1944–45* (New York: Knopf, 2008); Thomas W. Zeiler, *Unconditional Defeat: Japan, America, and the End of World War II* (Wilmington, DE: SR Books, 2004); and Stanley Weintraub, *The Last Great Victory: The End of the Pacific War, July/August 1945* (New York: Dutton, 1995). For an important edited collection that gathers together the work of such notable scholars as Richard B. Frank, Barton J. Bernstein, Sumio Hatano, and David Holloway see Tsuyoshi Hasegawa, ed., *The End of the Pacific War: Reappraisals* (Stanford: Stanford University Press, 2007). On the end of the war and its aftermath see Ronald H. Spector, *In the Ruins of Empire: The Japanese Surrender and the Battle for Postwar Asia* (New York: Random House, 2007).

The classic account of Japanese decision making at the end of World War II is Robert J. C. Butow, *Japan's Decision to Surrender* (Stanford: Stanford University Press, 1954). The story of the divisions within Japan over the surrender terms is told with dramatic flair in William Craig, *The Fall of Japan* (New York: The Dial Press, 1967). Sadao Asada provides an insightful Japanese perspective in "The Shock of the Atomic Bomb and Japan's Decision to Surrender – A Reconsideration," *Pacific Historical Review*, Vol. 67 (November, 1998), pp. 475–512. Also of notable importance are Herbert P. Bix, "Japan's Delayed Surrender: A Reinterpretation," *Diplomatic History*, Vol. 19 (Spring, 1995), pp. 197–225; Herbert P. Bix, *Hirohito and the Making of Modern Japan* (New York: HarperCollins, 2000); and Tristan Grunow, "A Reexamination of the 'Shock of Hiroshima': The Japanese Bomb Projects and the Surrender Decision," *The Journal of American-East Asian Relations*, Vol. 12 (Fall–Winter, 2008), pp. 155–189.

The controversy over the use of the atomic bomb shows no signs of ending. Recent works representing a variety of perspectives include: Tsuyoshi Hasegawa, *Racing the Enemy: Stalin, Truman, and the Surrender of Japan* (Cambridge, MA: Harvard University Press, 2005); Michael D. Gordin, *Five Days in August: How World War II Became a Nuclear War* (Princeton, NJ: Princeton University

Press, 2007); Sean L. Malloy, *Atomic Tragedy: Henry L. Stimson and the Decision to Use the Bomb Against Japan* (Ithaca, NY: Cornell University Press, 2008); Andrew Rotter, *Hiroshima: The World's Bomb* (New York and Oxford: Oxford University Press, 2008); and Campbell Craig and Sergey Radchenko, *The Atomic Bomb and the Origins of the Cold War* (New Haven, CT: Yale University Press, 2008). Stephen Walker, *Shockwave: Countdown to Hiroshima* (New York: HarperCollins, 2005) provides fascinating details. Robert James Maddox, ed., *Hiroshima in History: The Myths of Revisionism* (Columbia: University of Missouri Press, 2007) includes much of the best recent orthodox scholarship in an accessible way. D. M. Giangreco's *Hell to Pay: Operation Downfall and the Invasion of Japan, 1945–1947* (Annapolis, MD: U.S. Naval Institute Press, 2009) is a truly impressive work of military history that not only examines the military planning of the United States for the anticipated invasions of the Japanese home islands, but also details the unrelenting defensive preparations of Japan in its *Ketsu-Go* campaign. It constitutes essential reading for all those who truly want to comprehend Japan's defeat and the end of the Pacific War.

There is a large literature on the various individuals involved in the decisions regarding the use of the atomic bomb. Just some of the more important works can be noted here. Robert H. Ferrell's *Harry S. Truman: A Life* (Columbia: University of Missouri Press, 1994), emphasizes Truman's toughness and talents as a politician, and Alonzo Hamby's *Man of the People: A Life of Harry S. Truman* (New York: Oxford University Press, 1995), reveals a more complex Truman personality in compelling fashion. For Truman's own account see Harry S. Truman, *Memoirs,* Vol. 1, *Year of Decisions* (New York: Doubleday, 1955). On Secretary of War Stimson see Henry L. Stimson and McGeorge Bundy, *On Active Service in Peace and War* (New York: Harper and Brothers, 1948); and Godfrey Hodgson, *The Colonel: The Life and Wars of Henry L. Stimson, 1867–1950* (New York: Knopf, 1990). Secretary of State James F. Byrnes gave his account in two memoirs, *Speaking Frankly* (New York: Harper and Brothers, 1947); and *All in One Lifetime* (New York: Harper and Brothers, 1958). David Robertson's *Sly and Able: A Political Biography of James F. Byrnes* (New York: W.W. Norton, 1994) is very astute. Kai Bird and Martin Sherwin, *American Prometheus: The Triumph and Tragedy of J. Robert Oppenheimer* (New York: Knopf, 2005) won the Pulitzer Prize but should be used with considerable caution. Leslie R. Groves, *Now It Can Be Told: The Story of the Manhattan Project* (New York: Harper and Brothers, 1962) is typically forthright.

The development of postwar U.S. nuclear policy is traced very well in McGeorge Bundy, *Danger and Survival: Choices About the Bomb in the First Fifty Years* (New York: Random House, 1988). Also valuable are Gregg Herken, *The Winning Weapon: The Atomic Bomb in the Cold War, 1945–1950* (New York: Knopf, 1980), and Michael D. Gordin, *Red Cloud at Dawn: Truman, Stalin, and the End of the Atomic Monopoly* (New York: Farrar, Straus and Giroux, 2009).

On U.S.-Soviet relations at this time and the subsequent movement toward the Cold War see Wilson D. Miscamble, *From Roosevelt to Truman: Potsdam, Hiroshima, and the Cold War* (New York and Cambridge: Cambridge University Press, 2007). Also see John Lewis Gaddis's classic study The *United States and the Origins of the Cold War, 1941–1947* (New York: Columbia University Press,

1972); and Marc Trachtenberg's notably insightful *A Constructed Peace: The Making of the European Settlement, 1945–1963* (Princeton, NJ: Princeton University Press, 1999).

Michael Bess provides a thoughtful introduction to the ethical and moral dimensions surrounding the use of atomic bombs against Japan in his chapter "The Decision to Drop the Atomic Bomb: Twelve Questions" included in his *Choices Under Fire: Moral Dimensions of World War II* (New York: Knopf, 2006). The philosopher Elizabeth Anscombe's critical pamphlet "Mr. Truman's Degree," is reprinted in G. E. M. Anscombe, *The Collected Philosophical Papers of G. E. M. Anscombe*, Vol. III, *Ethics, Religion and Politics* (Oxford: Blackwell, 1981), pp. 62–71. McGeorge Bundy and Robert P. Newman give some attention to moral issues surrounding the bomb in their works previously mentioned. Bundy reacted specifically and thoughtfully to the criticisms of Michael Walzer in his *Just and Unjust Wars: A Moral Argument with Historical Illustrations* (New York: Basic Books, 1977).

Index

In this index a *p* following a page number denotes a photograph.